Arvo Pärt in Conversation

Arvo Pärt in Conversation

Enzo Restagno | Leopold Brauneiss | Saale Kareda
Arvo Pärt

Translated by Robert Crow

Dalkey Archive Press
Champaign | Dublin | London

ARVO PÄRT „PÄRT IM GESPRÄCH" UE 26300
© Copyright 2010 by Universal Edition A.G., Wien
English version by Dalkey Archive Press
© 2011 by Universal Edition A.G., Wien

Originally published in German as *Arvo Pärt Im Gespräch* by Universal Editions AG, 2010
Copyright © 2010 by Leopold Brauneiss, Saale Kareda, Arvo Pärt, Enzo Restagno
Translation copyright © 2012 by Robert Crow
First Dalkey Edition, 2012
All rights reserved

Library of Congress Cataloging-in-Publication Data

Arvo Pärt im Gespräch. English
  Arvo Pärt in conversation / Enzo Restagno, Leopold Brauneiss, Saale Kareda, Arvo Pärt
; translated by Robert Crow. -- First Dalkey edition.
    pages cm
  Includes bibliographical references and discography.
  Originally published: Arvo Pärt im Gespräch. Vienna : Universal Edition, 2010.
  ISBN 978-1-56478-786-6 (cloth : alk. paper)
  1. Pärt, Arvo--Interviews. 2. Composers--Estonia--Interviews. I. Restagno, Enzo, in-
terviewer. II. Brauneiss, Leopold, author. III. Kareda, Saale, 1968- author. V. Crow, Robert J., translator. VI. Pärt, Arvo, interviewee. VII. Title.
  ML410.P1755A7513 2012
  780.92--dc23
  [B]
                        2012029206

Supported by the Estonian Ministry of Culture and the Cultural Endowment of Estonia

Partially funded by a grant from the Illinois Arts Council, a state agency

www.dalkeyarchive.com

Printed on permanent/durable acid-free paper and bound in the United States of America

Contents

Foreword to the German Edition

Following the tradition of dedicating a comprehensive publication to each major composer featured at the Italian music festival Settembre Musica, the festival's artistic director, Enzo Restagno, brought out a book about Arvo Pärt, which was presented on the occasion of an extensive programme of the conductor's works in Turin in September 2004.

With this Universal Edition, we would like to make a large part of this important book, originally published in Italian, available to a German-speaking public. It represents an attempt to approach the conceptual world of the composer, his musical language, and his compositions, from a broad range of angles. With its varied choice of subject matter, the book is intended to appeal to readers from very different fields of interest.

Along with the extensive, highly personal conversations with Enzo Restagno that form its core, this volume includes an analytical essay by Leopold Brauneiss that requires rather more theoretical knowledge. This article is an important study of the theory and method behind Pärt's compositional intentions. The short essay by Saale Kareda is directed primarily toward those who are more interested in the spiritual aspects of Pärt's music.

Musicology today finds itself a little less at a loss in confronting the Pärt phenomenon than it did during the early years of his success. Yet few serious studies of his works have been undertaken. This book is intended to redress that deficit, at least in part. The compositional principle of "Tintinnabuli," upon which his works since 1976 have been based, is described in detail both by Leopold Brauneiss and Saale Kareda in the essays published here, and both pieces offer a valuable theoretical basis for further analytical, musicological study.

With the success of his music, public interest in the person of Arvo Pärt has, understandably, grown in recent decades as well—and until now, that interest has been but sparsely satisfied. Little that is well founded, and much that it purely speculative, has been written about Arvo Pärt—a state of affairs no doubt partly provoked by his own shyness in dealing with the media. He does not enjoy seeing himself at the centre of attention, and is always to be found one step behind his own music. Here, however, Arvo Pärt—as both composer and person—is at the centre of an extensive article by Enzo Restagno. Pärt and his wife Nora—who has stood at his side in all musical matters for 40 years—held lengthy conversations with Restagno in the summer of 2003, in the Italian Dolomites. Over the course of these interviews, Pärt describes his roots and his early life in Estonia during the days of the Soviet Union, his emigration, his artistic odyssey, his view of the world. These unique conversations took place in an atmosphere of great trust, and drew numerous, invaluable memories from the composer.

In closing, the appendix offers two acceptance speeches delivered by Pärt during the award ceremonies of two major composition prizes. Each of them offers an interesting view of Pärt's thinking, complementing the picture of composer and person in a very personal way.

The UE wishes to thank Enzo Restagno, Leopold Brauneiss, Saale Kareda, and of course Arvo and Nora Pärt, for placing these texts at our disposal for this publication.

UNIVERSAL EDITION
VIENNA, SEPTEMBER 2010

Arvo Pärt in Conversation

Enzo Restagno

ENZO RESTAGNO was born in Turin in 1941, and studied music and philoso-phy. He served as Professor of Music History for 37 years at the Giuseppe Verdi Conservatory in Turin, and was a music critic for numerous news-papers and magazines. He continues to give lectures and master classes in music institutions and universities throughout Europe, the USA, and Asia.

As a musicologist, Enzo Restagno has written books about Luigi Nono, Luciano Berio, Hanz Werner Henze, Elliot Carter, György Ligeti, Iannis Xenakis, Goffredo Petrassi, Franco Donatoni, Sofia Gubaidulina, Alfred Schnittke, Steve Reich, Louis Andriessen, Peter Maxwell Davies, Arvo Pärt, and finally, an internationally renowned book about Maurice Ravel.

During the last 25 years Enzo Restagno has been artistic director of the Symphony Orchestra of RAI (*Radiotelevisione italiana*) and of the Interna-tional Piano Festival *Arturo Benedetti Michelangeli* in Bergamo and Brescia. Since 1986 he has organised the festival *Torino Settembre Musica,* extended in 2007 to become the *MiTo Settembre Musica,* which has gone on to become one of the world's most prestigious international music festivals.

ENZO RESTAGNO: *From the biographical notes of your concert programmes, I learn that you were born in 1935 in Paide, Estonia, one of the Baltic States that until recently were part of the Soviet Union. I have always harboured a certain curiosity about that part of Eastern Europe—an area I have never visited, and about which, I have to admit, we know regrettably little here in Italy. When I think of those distant regions, the verses of T. S. Eliot occur to me: "Bin gar keine Russin, stamm' aus Litauen, echt deutsch,"[1] and I envisage the grey colour that, according to Theodor Storm, habitually enveloped his hometown on the Baltic coast. So I would be very grateful if you could tell us about those early years of your life, and conjure up something of the atmosphere of your birthplace, where I understand you lived only a short time, moving as you did with your mother to another Estonian town, Rakvere, when you were three years old.*

ARVO PÄRT: Paide lies in the centre of Estonia. It is a small town that hasn't changed much since the time of my earliest memories. Life flowed calmly and simply, more or less as it does here in Castel Tesino,[2] though Paide was perhaps a little larger. There was a small theatre in which I remember my parents used to perform. I once had a photograph of my father and mother standing on the stage during a performance. My father was a powerful, muscular man. In the picture he appears to be playing the role of a gladiator in Ancient Rome, or something like that. As you mentioned earlier, my mother moved with me very early on to a somewhat larger town, to Rakvere. This lies halfway between Tallinn—our capital city—and St. Petersburg. I remember that in the flat we moved into there was a grand piano of the make *S. Petersburg*. It wasn't a good instrument, but I played my first notes on it and used it until I was about seventeen years old. Looking back at my early life, I can see that I have forgotten a lot. Perhaps I was unable to retain all the details because, at the time, I paid too little attention to them. My parents separated before we moved from Paide. The son of our new landlord became my stepfather. The family I joined was particularly interesting. There were three brothers, the

---

1   "I'm not Russian at all, come from Estonia, genuine German." From T. S. Eliot's *The Waste Land*, where the sentence appears in German. (R.J.C.)
2   Castel Tesino is a mountain village in Trentino where these conversations took place in 2003 at the home of Silvia Lelli and Roberto Masotti—friends of Arvo Pärt. Also taking part were Nora Pärt and Nicola Davico, who assisted as a translator.

oldest was my stepfather, the second was a remarkably gifted musician who played the piano well and owned a well-stocked music library. The third was a very gifted draughtsman. When I think about it, I have to admit I was very lucky to end up in this milieu. The library proved very useful to me later on, though its owner, the musician, had since died.

If I'm not mistaken, a music school—the first in the town—was founded in Rakvere immediately after the end of the war. Since we already had a piano at home, my mother decided to send me to this school. That's how it all began.

E.R.: *You've told us about your family and your first encounter with music, but I'd like to learn something about the architecture of Rakvere: What did the buildings look like? What were they like inside? Could one detect a German influence or did they perhaps have specifically Estonian characteristics?*

A.P.: No, there was no specifically Estonian style. Such special features are only found in small rural villages. Estonian cities are basically no different from European cities. And you have to remember that Estonia had belonged to Germany for five centuries. Of course there was a certain Russian influence, but Rakvere was all in all just an ordinary town with low houses, mainly made of wood, and an old medieval centre with the ruins of a castle that is still much loved by children today, who meet there to play.

E.R.: *I assume you spoke the language of your mother—that is to say, Estonian—during your first years. Did you hear other languages, such as German or Russian?*

A.P.: At that time Estonia was a free country. The most frequently spoken language was Estonian. However, I remember the parents of my stepfather often spoke German or Russian. Their sons spoke German much more often, and hardly ever Russian. The Russian influence had diminished. My grandparents had travelled a lot during the time of the tsars, so they were familiar with the Russian culture and language. It's quite likely that the piano I mentioned earlier came into the family through some contact with the world of tsarist Russia. I can also remember the arrival of the Germans when I was five.

E.R.: *That was in 1941.*

A.P.: Yes, exactly, in 1941, when Estonia came under German control. When the war broke out, the soldiers who had spread through the whole town came and occupied every free space in people's flats. In ours as well. There were two or three of them, I'm not sure exactly how many. They moved into the room where the big piano stood. We played a lot of good music together, and we sang. All in all I can't claim that these were bad times. Bad things came later, from the East.

E.R.: *Exactly. In 1944 the Soviets arrived and stayed for fifty years. From that moment onward Estonia was part of the Soviet Union, albeit a very western part where a different language was spoken, as in East Prussia, which suffered the same fate. At the beginning of our conversation I said I would try to imagine the country by approaching it through related aspects of the neighbouring countries I know. I think of Königsberg, the town of Kant, which became Russian and was given the name Kalingrad. I think of Danzig with its melancholy atmosphere evoked so well by Günter Grass, and I think in general of all those parts of Eastern Europe, where in some cases I've travelled myself, but which for the most part I've visited only in my thoughts, guided by writers like Joseph Roth. When one grows up in this sort of region, I imagine, one must feel more open to a variety of influences, to other languages and cultures. You mentioned earlier that you heard three languages in your family, Estonian, German, and Russian. I am immediately reminded of what Elias Canetti tells us in Die gerettete Zunge,[3] namely that, as a child, the German language—the language of his parents—had seemed to him the language of culture.*

A.P.: In those days I could speak neither German nor Russian, and was unable to do so until I was ten. There was much confusion all around us—not just linguistic. One member of my family had been recruited by the Russian army and had to undergo the ordeal of a German concentration camp, while another, who had to serve in the German army, experienced the same thing on the other side. I was much too young, so I was spared such things. My

---

3   *The Tongue Set Free*

mother was also very protective. I saw this situation, with all its contradictions, through the eyes of a child. However, I can distinctly remember the burning houses and the people running to put them out. We were lucky—our house and the piano remained unharmed throughout the whole war.

E.R.: *You began very early with music, you were only seven years old. When and why did you decide to become a musician?*

A.P.: I can't really say. You are what you are, but nobody knows what he'll become—and certainly not a child. I can't honestly claim to have had the feeling then that I wanted to be a musician. But I believe that during my first attempts at composition a vague awareness did begin to take shape. Sometimes I imagine I had a premonition that, one day, I'd be able to compose and produce things like those that I heard on the radio or in concerts. But the truth is that I matured very late, and that back then I wasn't in a position to find the path that might have led me toward what I was really looking for. The great longing for such a path was later expressed by my exaggeratedly enthusiastic devotion to twelve-tone music. Then I distanced myself from it, because I was searching for something different. This was just one of many attempts to find my own way, my own world.

E.R.: *Yes, you're right: everyone is looking for their own particular path. One learns more day by day, gradually becoming convinced of one's own abilities, gaining self-confidence, and finally one decides to become a musician. However, the relationship to one's own family plays a large role in the decision to become a composer. In middle class society there's often a prejudice against music as a profession. It seems to me, however, that your family didn't oppose it in any way, presumably because they laid great importance upon a relationship with the arts.*

A.P.: Exactly, it was just as you say, though no one really supported my decision actively either. I can remember that I was reluctant to practice piano, and found it boring. At that time I didn't even know what it meant to be a composer. My mother followed my endeavours very attentively, and occasionally gave me a nut for my efforts. Times were hard, and there were no sweets. I tried to cut short all the tedious keyboard exercises, but sometimes, just for fun, extended them, and began something like improvisation.

E.R.: *As far as I know you learned not only piano but oboe and percussion as well. How did you come to learn these instruments?*

A.P.: It all happened very quickly and simply. In our school orchestra—every school had an orchestra—there was only one oboe player. One day a teacher thrust an oboe into my hand and said: "You can read music—get going!" I played the oboe terribly. After that I tried the flute, and I played percussion and piano alternately in a dance band. More or less gaining a command of these instruments proved very useful to me later on—not so much as a composer, more during military service. As a musician you had certain privileges: you weren't forced to cut your hair short, and you enjoyed better conditions. I played the oboe in the military band—Beethoven's *Coriolanus Overture* and pieces like that—but I never really mastered the instrument. Presumably because I never really applied myself to it. I remember that I played what notes I could manage much louder than everyone else. But in a military band that doesn't really matter, since everyone plays everything much too loud anyway. In the military band, on parade or at dances, I also played the bass drum and the side drum. What this experience taught me was that I had no sense of rhythm. When I grappled with the bass drum for the first time, all the other musicians stared at me in amazement, I remember that quite distinctly. I lost my place entirely and either played before or after the others. But the best of it was that I didn't notice. I thought *they* were all going wrong! In the end they said to me, "Didn't you notice?" I thought, "If I have to listen better, then I'll listen better." I no longer followed my own impulse, but theirs. And so I began to play to their rhythm. That taught me that one is capable of doing anything, if only one listens attentively enough. In the end I mastered the side drum, and even won the prize for best percussionist in a competition for military bands from all the Baltic states! Incredible!

E.R.: *If I understand correctly, you mean your sense of rhythm didn't correspond to that of the orchestra. How can you explain this discrepancy today? Was the rhythmic feeling of the orchestra too clumsy?*

A.P.: No, not at all too clumsy, they played quite correctly. Even today I probably wouldn't be able to conduct an orchestra. I would always be too early or too late, because I would be too busy thinking about what I had just heard. But I'd like to tell you about another experience from my time as a drummer. Once I had to play the side drum all on my own, and the whole battalion had to march to my beat. I didn't know what to do, because there was no other instrument that I could follow. So I said to myself: "They all march together, don't they, so I can rely on the rhythm of their own marching." This worked so well that I won the prize I just mentioned.

E.R.: *You mean that the soldiers' feet were the model you followed?*

A.P.: Absolutely! And that's not just an anecdote.

E.R.: *A little later, in 1953, Stalin died. The atmosphere that spread then throughout the entire Soviet Union has been described in Ilja Ehrenburg's novel* The Thaw. *The plot doesn't take place in Moscow or Leningrad, but in a distant provincial town. Was there something of this atmosphere of expectation and tentative hope to be felt in Tallinn?*

A.P.: Not at all. As far as I can remember we were all relieved that the danger and poverty had receded a little, but that was all.

NORA PÄRT: Perhaps it was also because you were only eighteen at the time, and at that age one has quite a different way of looking at things.

A.P.: Yes, that's probably true. I was in my second to last year at school, I was preoccupied with music, my family was really out of touch with these historical and political events, and our day-to-day life remained much the same. My mother was a kindergarten teacher—she remained one all her life—and my attention was focused entirely on music. At that time I attended the children's music school and these momentous events passed me by. They touched neither myself nor my teachers, since they weren't directly attached to the Party. Basically we lived in another dimension, we followed ideals that were not very different from those upon which our lives had been built before the Russian occupation. Naturally there was the hope that something would change, but by the time something actually did change we had long since moved to the West.

N.P.: Presumably my husband's generation was unable to fully realise the impact of the events of those years. They were too young and inexperienced, too bound up with their own artistic endeavours. Anyway, one mustn't forget that the communist era in Estonia lasted for a much shorter time than in the Soviet Union. That meant a shift in the perception of political reality: it was different, not so sharp and painful.

E.R.: *In the same year—that is, 1953—you moved to Tallinn to study at the Conservatory there. But shortly afterwards you had to leave to do military service, which in your case was relatively short, for health reasons. I came across this information in a biography, but the matter was only touched on in passing. This would be a good opportunity to expand on it further.*

A.P.: One day during my military service I felt a stabbing pain in my lower abdomen. The doctors suspected appendicitis, and operated on me. In fact it turned out just to be kidney colic, but as far as the military authorities were concerned, my health was permanently impaired. I was relieved of service and was allowed to return to the Conservatory.

E.R.: *Now I'd like to talk a little about your composition teacher Heino Eller. My research has left me with the impression that he was a truly noble musical personality with an exceptional, Russian-style education. I gather he studied violin with Leopold Auer and composition with Alexander Glazunov in Petersburg. You yourself have recorded some memories of Heino Eller. I would like to reproduce them here for the reader.*[4]

---

4   This text appears in the CD booklet to ECM New Series 1745—Heino Eller, *Neenia* (2001).

Memories of Heino Eller

I remember my composition teacher Heino Eller, and the years I spent studying with him, with much gratitude. I find it difficult to say what impressed me most: his manner of teaching or his personal charisma. The generosity and magnanimity of Heino Eller and his works have, over the decades, merged in my mind into an overall picture that has influenced me to this day. As a pedagogue he was invariably open to modern trends in the Arts. He allowed pupils to find their own way and respected their personal decisions, even if these sometimes differed from his own ideals. He imbued us with a sense of responsibility toward what we created, teaching us to remain true to ourselves. Heino Eller once said that his pedagogic goal was the development of each pupil's personality and individual musical language. The works of more than fifty pupils, from Eduard Tubin to Lepo Sumera, bear witness to this intention. His personality belonged to a different generation. Through it we came into contact with the pre-revolutionary aristocracy and its cultural heritage. Soviet ideology was unable to muddy his knowledge of human and cultural values. After his studies in St. Petersburg with its centuries-old tradition, he set quite new standards in the small country of Estonia and laid the foundation for professional music-making there. Characteristic of Heino Eller's oeuvre is its strict logic, cultivated stylistic sense, fine and masterful orchestration, and a highly-defined personal manner. These characteristics place him on a level with the great Nordic composers. One might say that Heino Eller's *Homeland Song* has achieved a symbolic character for Estonia similar to that of Sibelius's famous composition *Finlandia* in Finland. Now that I am the same age my teacher was then, I have come across a saying by Eller, one that I never heard him utter while he was teaching: "It is more difficult to find a single right note than to put a whole mass of them down on paper." Although he never talked about it, he obviously succeeded in anchoring the painful search for the one "right note" in my soul.

Arvo Pärt

A.P.: Heino Eller was much more than anything I can express in words. It is largely due to him that music in Estonia was able to achieve a cultural and professional dignity. He came from elevated social circles and his parents wanted him to enjoy an adequate cultural education, so they had him study law. It was only later that he moved to Petersburg to study violin and composition. Travelling was a great joy to him, and he travelled frequently. He had an insatiable interest in new currents in the arts, particularly if he could see in them a relationship to folk tradition. Yet he was also familiar with the music of Schoenberg and his school. Through him we were exposed to an incredible amount of music that he brought back from Western Europe. I believe he was at that time the only composer in Estonia who knew his way so thoroughly around the new music from the West. He was a good and gentle person, and as a teacher he always allowed his pupils room to develop in their own way. As a result his pupils became very different kinds of musicians.

E.R.: *I have always admired these sorts of noble teaching personalities, and over the course of my life I've had the luck to become personally acquainted with several: Goffredo Petrassi, who was an exceptional and compelling composition teacher at the Conservatorio di S. Cecila in Rome, and Olivier Messiaen from whose school many diverse and very gifted composers emerged. Earlier, in passing, you mentioned Heino Eller's interest in folkloric elements. Did your teacher pass this fondness on to you?*

A.P.: Unfortunately, I have to answer with a "no." Today I see things in a different light, but at the time something about it just didn't work. As I said, Eller never forced us to follow him. He limited himself to showing us how the folkloric material of Kodaly, Bartók, or Sibelius was employed in their music. The Hungarian and Finnish national schools lay very close to his musical sensibility, but I myself was not prepared to share his enthusiasm. I was much more taken by twelve-tone music, and I occupied myself zealously with the books of Herbert Eimert and Ernst Krenek. One of Eller's best pupils, Eduard Tubin, who had emigrated to Sweden, had given both of these treatises to him, and he used them for his lessons with us.[5]

---

5 This refers to Herbert Eimert *Lehrbuch der Zwölftontechnik*, (Weisbaden: Breitkopf

E.R.: *The atmosphere you enjoyed at the Conservatory in Tallinn was much freer than that which reigned in Moscow. Sofia Gubaidulina has described the oppressive atmosphere there, characterised by fear and denunciation, in which professors saw themselves constantly in danger of the accusation of Formalism. She also told me that Wissarion Schebalin got into a lot of trouble because he dared to show his pupils the score of Debussy's La Mer.*

A.P.: In a large city like Moscow every organization—schools included— were full of party functionaries, people watching everything that was going on, potential informants. In our Tallinn a similar structure was in place, but luckily it was not so efficient as in Moscow. And lessons with Eller took place not in the Conservatory but at his home, where the walls had neither ears nor eyes—for there were also informants among the students. Heino Eller was the oldest of the professors, he was much valued by everyone, and he and was a great moral authority. Other teachers—particularly teachers of music history—were more vulnerable to the system and had to suffer a great deal for their convictions. Music itself, however, was seen as a subject less susceptible to ideological influences, and so we were allowed to have lessons at home with Heino Eller without any trouble. His wife made biscuits for us, and one might almost say that for us each lesson was like a little party, because we were treated like private pupils.

N.P.: Eller often saved Arvo from bad marks, even in other subjects.

A.P.: Yes, that's right. I was having some difficulty with the counterpoint class. Eller heard about this, and said to his colleague, "All right, just leave him to me and I'll deal with it." He gave me valuable instruction and showed me simple tricks so effective that I was able to solve all my counterpoint exercises and finish off the programme for the whole year in a few weeks.

E.R.: *Who were the most important composers for Eller?*

& Härtel, 1952), and Ernst Krenek, *Studies in Counterpoint, Based On the Twelve-Tone Technique* (New York: G. Schirmer, 1940).

A.P.: Palestrina, whom we studied by way of the treatise by Knud Jeppesen.[6]

E.R.: *Palestrina—that would be for counterpoint, but who was the model for harmony?*

A.P.: Nikolai Rimsky-Korsakov and his book on harmony. I would like to tell you something else about Eller. As I said, he was a man of exceptional geniality, and I never heard him speak a harsh word to a student. He always corrected us with care and love, always with an eraser in his hand, in a manner that transformed reproach into encouragement. I also mentioned that he enjoyed great esteem and experienced no particular difficulties with the authorities. But when I think about it carefully, he did have one problem. He composed nothing but instrumental music, and that caused trouble because at that time all composers had to compose at least some music to texts in praise of the regime. Eller never did that, and in the end he came under suspicion. Luckily his pupils helped out and found some text that fit one of his quartets so well, one could have mistaken it for a vocal composition.

E.R.: *You've told us about your study of twelve-tone technique using the treatises of Herbert Eimert and Ernst Krenek that Heino Eller had got hold of from Sweden. Of course you somehow had to be able to cope with the general situation, but none the less, here you were, able to study undisturbed a serial technique that in Moscow was strictly forbidden. I remember Alfred Schnittke, Sofia Gubaidulina, and Edison Denisov telling me of the incredible difficulties they experienced in getting hold of a score, a record or any other form of documentation of this type of music. The study of contemporary music took place underground, predominantly by turning to a Rumanian musician Philipp Moisejevic Herscovici, who had been a pupil of Anton Webern and had been living for some time in Moscow unnoticed by any official institution. Nothing conveys the situation better that the words of Anna Akhmatova, describing the cultural situation in the Soviet Union: according to her one lived in a sort of*

---

6 The two standard works to which Arvo Pärt is referring are *Der Palestrinastil und die Dissonanz* (Lipzig: Breitkopf & Härtel, 1925), and *Kontrapunkt. Lehrbuch der klassischen Vokalpolyphonie* (Leipzig: Breitkopf & Härtel, 1935).

"pre-Gutenberg era," in which the most lively and up to date documentation circulated only in the form of homemade Samizdat.[7]

A.P.: I got to know Philipp Herscovici about ten years after Schnittke and Gubaidulina. He occasionally came to Tallinn, but I had no idea who he was. I even remember that he came to visit me, but I hadn't heard of him, and couldn't adequately appreciate his achievements. You see, in the big metropolises like Moscow, people had their lodestars that they could look up to, but in Tallinn everything had more modest, provincial dimensions. It's true, we weren't so oppressed, but we had to find our own ways of doing things, methods that were already in existence elsewhere—even if they'd been built up and disseminated in secret.

N.P.: The cultural practise of *Samizdat* was a very important phenomenon in the Soviet Union, a fertile ground for the generation that grew up with it, but in Estonia it was as good as nonexistent. Arvo did have contact with Alfred Schnittke, Sofia Gubaidulina, and other personalities of cultural life, but these were rather sporadic.

E.R.: *There is another parallel. Not only were twelve-tone music and other bold contemporary experiences forbidden in the Soviet Union, there was also exceptional scepticism towards pre-classical music, both baroque and early music. So in those years a movement for the rebirth of baroque music developed alongside new music that was studied in secret. Andrej Wolkonski founded the ensemble* Madrigal, *and Rudolf Barscjai founded the* Orchestra of Baroque Soloists. *A sort of return to Bach, so to speak, that distanced itself from the cult of symphonic form—a cult that was encouraged and nurtured by the ideologists due to its dialectic form, because it could be identified so readily with the rules of Marxist thought. The parallel that I want to draw is between this Bach-renaissance in the Soviet Union on the one hand, and the Bach-worship that characterizes your earliest important works, the* Collage on B-A-C-H *for example or* Pro et Contra.

---

7   A widespread practise of disseminating non-conformist writing through self-publication in unofficial channels.

A.P.: The relationship between my works and Bach's music has rather different roots. Turning to Bach was for me a way of stating my position regarding my experience with twelve-tone music. I wanted to step outside the situation, in order to step into something that I had not yet explored. In my state of extreme discomfort at that time I wanted to prove to myself how beautiful Bach's music was, and how hateful mine was. What I am saying may sound odd, but I was convinced that through this musical sacrifice I could gain a clearer vision of my own contradictions. Works like *Credo* for piano, choir, and orchestra, and *Collage on B-A-C-H,* are conceived within a strict mathematical structure, as a play between black and white—that is why in *Credo* I only used notes corresponding to the white keys, as in the first prelude of Bach's *Well Tempered Clavier.* I could have chosen other material for the development of my theme, but what interested me at that moment was the colour white.

E.R.: *You said that you used material from Bach in order to emancipate yourself from the dodecaphonic technique. I would like to retrace those first steps with you. One of your first compositions based on the principles of twelve-tone music was* Nekrolog, *a piece you wrote in 1960 in Moscow that was performed with exceptional success in Moscow, Leningrad, and Zagreb. However, this piece did not only bring success, but many problems as well. I have here a quote in which you say the following: "My life has always been full of restlessness. It all started in 1960 when I composed my first piece for orchestra,* Nekrolog. *I was a student at the conservatory in Tallinn at the time and wrote the piece according to the principles of twelve-tone music—something that was very unusual for the time and the place. As a result, I suffered relentless criticism from elevated cultural circles, because nothing was felt to be more hostile than Western influence, to which twelve-tone music also belonged." You said before that you were dissatisfied with your music at that time, but when I think of your* Perpetuum mobile *from the year 1963 I cannot understand the reasons behind your dissatisfaction.* Perpetuum mobile, *which enjoyed resounding success at the Warsaw festival, is a piece that only lasts 4 minutes and radiates nothing but a positive quality of sound. Formally it is written using twelve-tone technique, but the resulting sound seems to belong to a different spirit, a little in the manner of Ravel or Ligeti.*

A.P.: I find it hard today to talk about things that happened such a long time long ago. But I can assure you that the world I carried within myself was riddled which such deep cracks that in comparison the atmosphere and language of twelve-tone music seemed more pleasant. That is, of course, just one side of the coin. *Perpetuum mobile* lacks any trace of aggression—in it there are other ideas and other ideals that transmit their own sort of cheerful experience.

N.P.: Might we describe it as twelve-tone music with a human face?

A.P.: Yes, or perhaps the picture of an extraterrestrial world would be more fitting, one in which human suffering has been eliminated in order to make room for a more objective and distanced view of things. In *Nekrolog* this isn't the case, each single note is written as if with a fist clenched in protest—a protest of which there is not a trace in *Perpetuum Mobile*.

E.R.: *And one recognises in this piece a feature that was to become characteristic of your style. The piece grows out of silence, there is an effective crescendo, then one returns again to silence.*

A.P.: At that time I was convinced that every mathematical formula could be translated into music. I thought that in this way one could create a more objective and purer kind of music. If I had succeeded by other means in creating a music free of emotion, I would have been able to distance myself from twelve-tone music. *Perpetuum mobile* rose out of a mathematical and philosophical idea, and was intended to represent a spiral path that reaches the point where it started, albeit on another level.

E.R.: *If I'm not mistaken* Perpetuum mobile *is dedicated to Luigi Nono. How did this dedication come about?*

A.P.: For us, the chance of coming into contact with a young composer from the West was an exceptional experience. Luigi was also very affectionate and cordial towards us, even though we could not cultivate our relationship with him as we would have liked. But in Tallinn, we in the Composers Society were allowed to hear some of his compositions.

E.R.: *I was a close friend of Luigi Nono and perhaps you'll be pleased to know that some years ago I had a long conversation with him in Berlin, just like the one I'm having with you now, which grew into a published book.*

A.P.: Just imagine, we were in Berlin at that time too!

E.R.: *It's good to hear about your friendship. There aren't many of us aboard this fragile ship of contemporary music, and these friendships express more than a sense of solidarity. I have come to know many living composers, have occupied myself with their works, and it has gradually become clear to me that all these experiences, even if they are very different or even contradictory, in the end make up a coherent picture, a picture of the time that we've lived through—and they do so better than any history book. But let's return to Luigi Nono. I'd like to learn something of your re-lationship with him, not just when you were in Tallinn, but also later on in Berlin.*

A.P.: In Berlin we only met a few times at our home. It's difficult to talk about him. He had changed very much over the years. He was, as you know, a fighter by nature, if one may say so, a true communist. In Russia however he was viewed as an anti-communist. Often people were interrogated by KGB agents about their relationship to Nono.

E.R.: *I know that his visits were seen as being dangerous.*

A.P.: Yes, very dangerous, but we were too fascinated by his personality to worry about that.

E.R.: *When Nono travelled to Moscow it was no doubt Thikon Khrennikov who worried the most.*

A.P.: Nono always expressed himself with great directness, and said quite openly that Soviet culture and politics were a quagmire. Once he said to Khrennikov of all people: "You and your communism are stuck in a quagmire!" But later on in Berlin he became more moderate. I must admit, his admiration for Gorbachev surprised me a lot.

N.P.: Nono was so incredibly likeable, an eternal teenager that had yet to discover the world. Because communist ideals had been shattered, he was forced to look for something else. He was a utopian.

A.P.: Yes, a true utopian. He also had a great interest in Russian religious philosophy.

E.R.: *In his later years he distanced himself from the communist party line and was heavily criticised for this. He loved the poetry of Hölderlin, in which he saw a secret map of the development of musical language and thought. For him it was a very normal development.*

Now I'd like to return to the relationship between your music and the music of Bach. In 1964 you wrote Collage on B-A-C-H *for strings, oboe—perhaps a reminiscence of your experience as oboist—cembalo and piano. It is a composition in which one clearly senses a desire for closure with its own musical past. This becomes apparent as soon we see the way in which the three movements—* Toccata, Sarabande, *and* Ricercar *are realised. The Sarabande—in a manner that was surely unusual at the time—consists of an instrumentation of Bach's Sixth Suite in D-minor, whereas* Pro et Contra, *which came about through a commission from Mstislav Rostropovich, employs baroque and serial elements in alternation. Did this juxtaposition really prove fertile?*

A.P.: One can see it as a mixture of positive and negative, true and false. The *Collages* are a sort of transplantation: if you have the feeling that you don't have a skin of your own, you try to take strips of skin from all around you and apply them to yourself. In time these strips change, and turn into a new skin. I didn't know exactly where this experiment of the *Collages* would lead me, but in any case I had the impression I was carrying a living organism in my hands, a living substance, such as I had not yet found in twelve-tone music. I realised that another world existed, one that exercised a strong attraction on me—a world I would not have reached through twelve-tone technique. But one cannot go on for ever with the method of transplantation. In *Credo* the collage technique reaches its limits. It is as if one finds oneself in a cul-de-sac. In order to go on one has to break through the wall. For me, this happened through the conjunction of several, often accidental, encounters. One of these, which in retrospect turned out to be of great importance, was with a short piece from the Gregorian repertoire that I heard quite by chance for a few seconds in a record shop. In it I discovered a world that I didn't know, a world without harmony, without metre, without timbre, without instrumentation, without anything. At this moment it became clear to me which direction I had to follow, and a long journey began in my unconscious mind.

N.P.: In a music "without anything," the central question is: what path a single note takes in order to merge into the next. That is at the core of the whole work.

A.P.: Yes, but it wasn't until later that I realised one can express more with a single melodic line than with many. At that time, given the condition in which I found myself, I was unable to write a melodic line without numbers; but the numbers of serial music were dead for me as well. With Gregorian Chorale that was not the case. Its lines had a soul.

E.R.: *Allow me to change the subject a little: when we spoke of your relationship to Bach, I was reminded of Stravinsky and his neoclassical experience. However, in your treatment of the material you proceed in quite a different way. One could never accuse you of being neoclassical.*

A.P.: It would be interesting to learn the reasons that led Stravinsky to realise his project. Perhaps he too felt the need for old colours, past epochs.

E.R.: *Perhaps one should speak of contours and profiles instead of colours?*

A.P.: Yes, I believe "profile" would be appropriate. Perhaps Stravinsky also felt a nostalgia for those past times, for the ideals of a past epoch.

E.R.: *An attempt to awaken the experiences of the past to life, a reluctance to admit that they are gone for good . . .*

A.P.: I believe he felt at home in this music. His love found its true expression there.

N.P.: Stravinksy once said that no one can feel at home in modern music, because in times of linguistic crisis one is constantly in search of something. Nevertheless, the experiences of the *Collage on B-A-C-H* and indeed some works of Schnittke were very different. In the *Collage on B-A-C-H* an explosive collision of two worlds takes place. The deep inner conflict mirrored within it led finally, in *Credo*, to real musical auto-aggression.

A.P.: The *collages* of Shostakovich, and in some cases of Schnittke too, have quite a different character. They are "grotesque" and spring from ideals that I cannot quite describe, though without a doubt they exist. For my part I wanted to show the nakedness of this emperor of twelve-tone music, as in Anderson's tale about the emperor's new clothes, where only a child has the innocence and courage necessary to reveal his nudity.

E.R.: *Could you explain the difference between your position and that of so called* grotesque *composers like Schnittke?*

A.P.: Probably not, but I can tell you that my *collages* have often been misunderstood and treated as *grotesque*. Critics content themselves by saying that these compositions are interesting, that they are skilfully written and the like, but such works are a genuine part of myself.

N.P.: At the end of the *Second Symphony* you quote Tchaikovsky. Critics took this as an ironic reference, but that is not the case. The Tchaikovsky quote is central to the work. Here childlike innocence and tenderness are juxtaposed with the cruelty of the outside world, and it is the tender side that comes out as the winner. If it is regarded just as a joke the whole work is ruined.

E.R.: *One has to admit that some critics have utterly misinterpreted many important works. Of course I am also thinking of Schnittke, who justified the use of classical themes in his works (for example* Moz-Art à la Haydn) *by claim-*

ing he conceived the music in a dream. Stravinksy said the same thing, and a statement like this basically bears out what you said earlier—that Stravinksy wanted to relive his passion for this old music.

A.P.: Obviously. Why else did he have to compose so much of his music in Venice? Presumably because he felt at home there. This milieu made up a large part of his world.

E.R.: *In the early Sixties you worked for a time for Estonian Radio. I assume you were employed as an ordinary technician, but this work must have given you the opportunity to hear a lot of music. What was this period like for you?*

A.P.: This work took place parallel to my studies at the Conservatory. As a sound technician I had very flexible hours. We made recordings—three to four hours a day—or we broadcast live concerts. It was interesting work. Through it I gained access to recordings of all possible types of music, but most of all I got to see and hear a large number of scores of contemporary music. At Estonian Radio almost all of the sound technicians were composers—alongside me worked Eino Tamberg, Heino Jürisalu, Jaan Koha, Jaan Rääts, later Lepo Sumera joined us—and together we formed a very lively and creative group. One of the most valuable sides of our work lay in the musical exchange with other countries, not so much with Germany, France, or Italy, but places like the former Czechoslovakia, Hungary, or Poland, from which we were exposed to very interesting music. The result of this exchange was not always well-received by Estonian Radio's listeners, but it did give us the opportunity of approaching this "forbidden music" that otherwise lay locked away in the archives.

E.R.: *Could you give us some examples of this forbidden music? Was it by composers of the Eastern Bloc, or other composers?*

A.P.: No, others as well.

E.R.: *You mean music by Boulez's, Nono, Stockhausen, Berio, to name just a few?*

A.P.: Yes, some of their compositions were among the "forbidden" music, but the main source of new music for us came from Moscow, through the mediation of Schnittke and Denisov. Both of them also had personal connections to many composers in the West, to Pierre Boulez for example, and so it happened that compositions that were censored in Moscow did come to us.

E.R.: *During these years, in spite of all the official guidelines, there was a lively exchange of information, fed by the most varied of channels. I clearly remember Luigi Nono telling me how he used to bring a great many scores and records for his friends on his visits to Moscow. There was also the festival of the* Warsaw Autumn *that acted like a sort of free zone, to which musicians from the East could go without great difficulty to hear the voices of their colleagues in the West. Which works that actually could evade the censor were of particular interest to you?*

A.P.: I would say that everything interested me, without exception. We did not differentiate between good and bad with this music. In our Soviet ghetto we were happy to accept everything that came from the outside. Only time would tell in which direction each individual composer was going to move, and Edison Denisov, for example, chose quite a different path than I did. But that only became clear as the years went by. At the time we accepted everything with great respect, and if you really want to hear about my own favourites I would have to mention Anton Webern. Somebody—I don't know who—succeeded in bringing a recording of the complete works of Webern and managed to let our radio station get hold of it. I assure you, this music made a very strong impression on me. At this time I had already had the opportunity of hearing Boulez' music, but that for my ears was fairly exotic. The music of Webern on the other hand touched me deeply, probably because of its great transparency.

E.R.: *With all the illegal music that was circulating did you also have the opportunity of hearing Messiaen?*

A.P.: No, I don't recall that I did. With a few exceptions we felt ourselves drawn to the music of our own generation. Looking back, I would like to stress how much these decisions surprise me now—individual choice and personal favourites apart.

As soon as we started to write different music, influenced by Western models, we were stamped as enemies of the party and were persecuted. When I came to the West I discovered that the very same composers that I had taken as models, and because of whom I had been accused of being a friend of capitalism, were trying with their own compositions to fight *against* capitalism. I thought about this paradoxical situation, and it became clear to me that the world of New Music carried within itself the germ of conflict. Do you want to know why I distanced myself from this music? I did it because for me by this time these conflicts had lost their power, and with it their meaning. One might say that I had come to terms with myself and with God—and in so doing, all personal demands on the world had receded into the background.

E.R.: *I find this idea of New Music as the carrier of conflicts very interesting. I would be grateful if you could go into it in more detail.*

A.P.: It is purely a personal matter. I have come to recognise that it is not my duty to struggle with the world, nor to condemn this or that, but first and foremost to know myself, since every conflict begins within ourselves. That does not mean that I am indifferent, but if someone wants to change the world then he must begin with himself. I am absolutely convinced of this. If one does not begin with oneself, every step towards the world will be nothing but a big lie and at the same time an attack, and this hidden aggressiveness tends to go on spreading. How to do this is quite a different story, but if one starts off with this idea, everything else appears in a new light. And so I set off in search of new sounds. In this way the path itself becomes a source of inspiration. The path no longer runs outwards from us, but inwards, to the core from which everything springs. That is what all my actions have come to mean: building and not destroying.

E.R.: *The question that I would like to ask you now is related to your film music. You have composed a good deal for films, and occasionally for the theatre too. In my opinion this is an important experience for a composer, because it offers an opportunity to gain greater competence in describing situations and atmospheres.*

A.P.: While in the West film composers are specialists, in the Soviet Union composers such as Prokofiev and Shostakovich wrote music for films. This was mainly due to the political situation in Russia at the time. In films it was more difficult to censor music, and there was effectively no censor for film music at all. Dialogue and pictures were regularly cut out, but no one seemed to be interested in the musical background. Much of Schnittke's music that was otherwise forbidden in the concert hall could be used without a problem in film. With us in Estonia the situation was very similar—to be more exact, better than in Moscow—because everything that we wrote could be performed somehow. I remember one of Luigi Nono's visits to Tallinn. We went to the cinema together to see a film for which I had written the music. I had composed pieces that one might describe as dodecaphonic jazz, for saxophone, vibraphone, and trumpet. If I had presented them in the context of a chamber music concert, I would have had great difficulties. Luigi Nono was very amused by this too.

N. P. Film music was an opportunity to express oneself in music with complete freedom. As well as film music Arvo composed a lot of music for children's theatre.

A.P.: That's right! In film music there was that liberating creative atmosphere—almost like an improvisation—that could never be used in my compositions, where everything is strictly structured. One mustn't forget however that for many composers—including Schnittke, Denisov, and Sofia Gubaidulina—film music was their only source of income. So called pure music—symphonies, quartets, and the like—could only bring in money in the case of a state commission.

E.R.: *Alfred Schnittke and Sofia Gubaidulina told me the same thing a few years ago. What I find most pitiful about that climate of repression is that the list of guidelines wasn't put together by Thikon Khrennikov alone. Many others worked on it too, including mediocre and reactionary composers who, by doing so, secured their own privileges and struck a blow at their more talented colleagues. To believe that belonging to the select circle of artists—or as romantics would say, the "beautiful souls"—implies a certain amount of magnanimity, would be naive. I don't want to wander too far off the subject, and I will re-*

strict myself to naming those Russian composers of the old school such as Aram Khachaturian, Dmitry Kabalevsky, and Georgy Sviridov, who received all the major jobs and lucrative commissions. These were much-honoured musicians, who were in some cases gifted but who were predominantly engaged in keeping other composers from getting at their own privileges. The problem is that the law of divide et impera *applies as much to the management of a shop as it does to the government of any regime. But let's return to your works of the Sixties. I'd like to talk about a short composition that had immense success, namely* Solfeggio, *which you wrote in 1963.*

A.P.: I am not quite sure what there is to say. It is simply a scale (C-D-E-F-G-A-B-C) that takes the form of a four-part cluster, in that every note is sustained into the following note. In this composition I was following the tracks of *Perpetuum mobile,* but I was only using seven notes, and no longer twelve. As you can see, the basic idea was very simple, and I didn't know if it would work before I heard the result.

E.R.: *But in fact it works very well.*

A.P.: Yes, if it is performed properly.

E.R.: *In the meantime—we are still talking of the Sixties—you had written two symphonies. What can you tell us about these two compositions?*

A.P.: I always find it hard to talk about my own works. Sometimes I cannot imagine that I could comment on them at all. My first symphony was the final work for my diploma at the conservatory. It is a modest dodecaphonic composition. The second was a little more complicated. It is the first work in which I attempt to place black and white in opposition.

E.R.: *Are you saying that you wanted to give this technique a human face?*

A.P.: I wouldn't be so radical—I'd say that what I realised in practical terms with this symphony was simply the attempt to find out where I might feel more at home. Today I am more tolerant, towards this style as well. It isn't the fault of the twelve notes themselves. It all depends on the composer and how he uses those twelve notes. It depends on whether he wishes to produce poison or honey. Webern for example never produced poison. There are clear boundaries for the use of every material; primarily one must understand how any system can be induced to bear fruit. Often it is the system itself which teaches us how we should approach it and use it. But I was far less tolerant in those days, and I went through the experience of my second symphony and the *Credo* with a good deal of nervousness. I had the feeling that I could not afford to be the least bit careless.

E.R.: *There is a very important work you wrote in 1968: the* Credo *for piano, choir, and orchestra. The première took place together with a performance of Stravinsky's* Symphony of Psalms *in Tallinn, conducted by Neeme Järvi. As far as I know it was a scandalous success. Scandals are often very advantageous to a composer's career, but what I find remarkable in this case is that the outrage was caused by the central section of the piece, of all places. Here the dodecaphonic technique is used with serial processes and peaks in a mighty mimesis of chaos. I would like to hear from the composer himself what intentions lay behind this score.*

A.P.: At that time, and perhaps a little earlier, I felt as if I was on the brink of discovering something I might call a new beginning. The most important aspect of my work on the new piece turned out to be the text that I wanted to set. It concerns that passage of the Gospel where the teachings of Christ are most clearly felt—the point where Jesus answers the Old Testament's *Oculum pro oculo, dentem pro dente (an eye for an eye, a tooth for a tooth)* with the words: *Autem ego vobis dico: non esse resistendum injuriae (But I say unto you that you should not resist evil)*. I literally broke this sentence down into numbers and letters, so that each word corresponded to the orchestral means I employed. I'd like to describe the circumstances under which the work arose. It was customary in the Soviet Union that a composer should present any new work to a commission, whether in the form of a rehearsal of the work or a recording. The commission would then decide whether the work was suitable to be performed publicly or not. I did not have a recording of the piece, so I invited some members of the commission to the dress rehearsal.

As fate would have it, the most merciless member of the commission, the only zealous party activist and my arch-enemy, fell ill precisely on this day. I explained to those who heard my *Credo* that I had used material taken from the first prelude of Bach's *Well-Tempered Clavier*. This made them feel happy, and they thought the text was completely harmless, presumably because it was in Latin. The piece was indeed accepted and came to be performed. On that night, the audience was so enthusiastic that the conductor had the *Credo* played again from beginning to end, but the exuberant reaction of the audience aroused the first doubts within the commission, and they began to suspect that the piece contained subversive elements. I remember that a few days after the performance we travelled with the *Credo* to a congress in Moscow. I was part of a very large delegation. The president of the cultural commission was there too, and no one spoke a single word to me, because the memory of the scandal was still too vivid. But then I was accosted in the corridor of the train by the rather tipsy chief of the delegation, who smiled at me secretively and let a piece of paper peep out of his jacket pocket, upon which I could catch a fleeting glimpse of the Latin text of the credo of the mass. This was intended as an unambiguous hint that they had caught me out. In fact, apart from the first word, my *Credo* had nothing to do with the credo of the mass at all! But I got the message that the situation was serious and that investigations were already underway at the highest level. After this happened I was interrogated several times, and the interrogators repeated the same question over and over again: "What political aim are you pursuing in this work?"

N.P.: And they added, "And do not forget that this work must never again be performed and you must not offer it to anyone else." Intimidations and provocations followed, but in hindsight I have the impression that we weren't really aware of the seriousness of the situation. There is one other important detail that Arvo has forgotten to emphasise: the dodecaphonic section is based on fifths.

A.P.: Yes, it is. I constructed the dodecaphonic framework by setting a succession of fifths—the most pure and harmless of intervals—one after another to a point of maximum orchestral expansion. Through this juxtaposition of fifths the piece achieves an increasingly dense texture, a real saturation of sounds that acts as a representation of chaos and destruction. Only then do we hear Jesus' words: "But I say unto you . . . ," and so everything falls apart into its constituent parts. It is like the breakup of the Soviet regime, someone may have interpreted it that way and been afraid.

N.P.: At the end of the year there was a sort of opinion poll in the local press. People were asked to name the most impressive cultural event in which they had taken part. Ninety per cent of those questioned named this concert.

E.R.: *Thank you for that passionate description of the* Credo *and its consequences. What you say just goes to show how skilful the censor actually was in tracking down potential subversive threats. To imagine that the censors were uneducated and clumsy, and therefore not in a position to notice subtle intentions hidden behind any work of art, is in my opinion unforgivable naïveté. But let's return to your career, which, after the remarkable première of the* Credo, *began to take shape for the first time. Until 1968 you had used the dodecaphonic method, albeit without great strictness. These compositions reflect that typical unease of someone who has not yet found his own solution to his problems. After these somewhat torturous essays there followed a long period of silence, during which an original perspective finally emerged. I am aware that it may be awkward for you to reconstruct the path you followed during this silent period, but for our work, and for all those reading this book, it's too valuable an opportunity to miss.*

A.P.: At the time I was convinced that I just could not go on with the compositional means at my disposal. There simply wasn't enough material to go on with, so I just stopped composing altogether. I wanted to find something that was alive and simple and not destructive. When I worked at the radio I was allowed to deal with the most elaborate and powerful electronic equipment, such as loudspeakers and tape recorders. Suddenly however I felt the need to distance myself from this luxury, because I had the feeling that I was locked in a gilded cage and was being forced in the wrong direction. If I had to work with technical equipment I always chose the most simple, for example a simple tape recorder that offered just the basics. I was no longer at all interested in the adjustment of high and low frequencies, reducing the noise level and so on. What I wanted was only a simple musical line that lived and breathed inwardly, like those in the chants of distant epochs, or such as still exist today in folk music: an absolute melody, a naked voice which is the source of everything else. I wanted to learn how to shape a melody, but I had no idea how to do it.

All that I had to go on was a book of Gregorian chant, a *Liber usualis*, that I had received from a church in Tallinn. When I began to sing and to play these melodies I had the feeling that I was being given a blood transfusion. It was terribly strenuous work because it was not simply a matter of absorbing information. I had to be able to understand this music down to its very roots: how it had come into existence, what the people were like who had sung it, what they'd felt during their lives, how they'd written this music down and passed it on through the centuries until it became the source of our own music. In some way or other I succeeded it getting into contact with this music. But I never used this closeness as a quote, with the exception of one early piece that I wrote for Bologna Cathedral: *Statuit ei Dominus*. In Gregorian chant the succession of notes forms something like real speech, the notes offer concrete information, something that is comparable to birdsong. We do not understand them, but they understand each other. Monodic music has a certain informal content, it has arisen like a cathedral from ground that bears within it the ruins of earlier temples, probably a heathen temple that in its turn was erected in early pre-history on that site for quite specific reasons. This chain of forms, temples, and chants, each built upon the ruins of the other, is something more potent than we can imagine. In my daily work, too, I came up against tremendous difficulties. For a time I succeeded in writing a single musical line, but then I didn't know how to go on. Should I have written just monodic music? What would have become of polyphony and harmony? What should I have done with the second and third voice? Where should a second voice come from? Tormented by these questions, I began to think about the beginnings of polyphony. It became clear to me that it was far more complex and profound than the rigid rules with which Knud Jeppesen had analysed and explained this music would have us suppose. The second voice must be something independent, like the husband and wife in a family. This relationship of independent parts can, in my opinion, already be seen in the beginnings of ancient polyphony. I tried to realise this intuition in my third symphony where I conceived the entire form of the composition through the metaphor of the building of a town: small, increasingly numerous centres that spread out until they touch each other and form a unity. The same thing happens with the harmonic progression in the piece that is evolved from a series of short cadences. Upon this idea is based the idea of polyphonic complexity. Nonetheless, my experience with the third symphony left me dissatisfied. It became clear to me that I was caught within my relationship to musical history, which was too much one of debt. And that my work somehow lacked a style of its own. But I had succeeded in building a bridge within myself between yesterday and today—a yesterday that was several centuries old—and this encouraged me to go on exploring. During those years I filled thousands of pages with exercises in which I wrote out single voiced melodies. At home there is a cupboard full of exercises like this.

N.P.: What he was trying to do was to create a new way of hearing. That was why he didn't listen to any other sort of music during this period. Arvo wanted to find this mysterious source within himself and let the sounds flow freely out. He tried to gather all the information that might be helpful towards this end. He would read psalms, and immediately afterwards try to write a melodic line without a break, without control, as if he was blind, in order to be able to transform the impressions of his reading immediately into music.

A.P.: Yes, I read a psalm and filled a whole page, without thinking much about it, in the hope that there might be some sort of connection between what I read and what I wrote. Then I got on with reading the next psalm. I'm sure that between the psalm and my melody there was no connection at all. At least I didn't notice any. However I still hoped for some sort of osmosis, and so I went on and repeated the same process with one hundred and fifty psalms.

N.P.: Arvo wanted to develop his spontaneity, and not just through this experiment with the psalms—I can remember that he observed flocks of birds, sketched them in a book, and wrote a melody next to the drawing. In other cases he used photos of mountains as inspiration to find a musical phrase. He had the feeling that the observation of cold, dead rules from years gone by had extinguished his own free, creative impulse.

Now he was trying to rediscover it. It's interesting to note that Arvo later imposed rules upon himself again, albeit of quite a different kind.

A.P.: Yes, that is true enough. With the tintinnabuli style I went back to rules.

N.P.: You can't imagine how important this period was, with all its pages of exercises and psalms. He didn't know if he had found anything at all, and if he had, what it was. But he would certainly have given up composition if he had found nothing. I was very worried about him, and saw how much he was suffering. I knew that he would not have been able to go on living without that music, which was the real content of his life. I saw that he was about to implode, and didn't know if he would manage to bring these labour pains to a happy conclusion.

E.R.: *What you're saying is incredible—almost like an old fairy tale in which, somewhere or other, magic has a part to play. If you'll allow me to make a personal comment: the way you experience your relationship to time—particularly the time of waiting—impresses me deeply.*

A.P.: Anyway, I can tell you that it's during our times of waiting that we discover we have time at all.[8] But, returning to our point, I don't know how a second voice came to be added, but I do know that it happened in quite a different context than that of the old polyphony. Perhaps I might say that in earlier polyphony, 1+1 equals 1+1, while in my music 1+1 equals 1. There two notes are two realities, each different from one another; in my music they become one single thing.

N.P.: I might compare the moment when Arvo came to introduce the second voice to the moment of the creation of the world. It was like an enormous explosion, a discovery whose potential has yet to be fully realised. Arvo fought for almost ten years to be able to write a melodic line, but in the end he recognised that he could not go on, because one line was not enough. It's the

---

8   During the course of these conversations, Arvo Pärt emphasises this "We have time" with a forcefulness and urgency that lends the expression a certain celebratory quality.

same as flying: you need a pair of wings. Two lines were necessary to allow the melodies to take off.

All music lives from certain fields of tension. Traditional music is based on tonal harmonic, functional harmonic tensions that hold the whole musical material together. In Arvo's music the necessary tension is reached through minute vertical layerings: the upper melodic voice moves freely in the tonal universe, principally in stepwise motion, and is thus clearly audible as tonal harmony. The second voice moves only within the area of three notes, whereby only a single function, that of the tonic is emphasised. In this way a sort of tension arises between both voices that, on the one hand, complement each other, and on the other hand polarise—as with electricity, there is a negative and positive pole. It is like a continuous field of tension between a dynamic and a static state, as if one had fused normally exclusive dynamic and static fields into a unity.

A.P.: Basically the tintinnabuli concept represents something comparable to what normally happens when one begins to learn the piano: with the left hand one plays always the same chord while the right hand develops the melody. In my case there is a melody and three notes, but each note of the melody is bound to one of the three notes according to very exact rules and, naturally, *vice versa*. Obviously, unexpected dissonances arise, but there is a logic in the upper voice as there is also in the three notes that accompany it—albeit a hidden logic. That is the melodic dichotomy I referred to with my equation $1+1=1$.[9] In *Cantus*, for example, there are five melodic lines and each of them has its corresponding tintinnabuli line. The technical principle is that on the basis of the same rules many possibilities for the accompaniment of the voices arise. Accordingly this second voice is not a free harmonic voice but follows the melodic line. In the way a child resembles its parents, the tintinnabuli voice carries the gene of the melody within it. Perhaps I could say that the melodic voice represents my sins and imperfections while the second voice is the forgiveness afforded me. In this case my subjective faults are corrected. I would like to add that in this way I have also tried to give a higher degree of objectivity to the melodic voice—especially in vocal

---

9   This point is expanded upon in the essays by Saale Kareda and Leopold Brauneiss.

works, in that each word used in the music can be grasped by all musical parameters. There are very many possibilities of setting words to music, but for me the text with all its parameters is the basis of the musical structure.

E.R.: *Thank you for this explanation of the tintinnabuli style. I have read a great deal on the subject and I must admit that the metaphysical attributes—which I instinctively rather distrust—have tended to alienate me. On the other hand, the interpretation that something of a healing complementarity exists between objective and subjective dimensions in the interplay of the two voices, seems very significant. Nora is right when she says that the potential contained within the intuition of the tintinnabuli style is far from having been fully realised, and I believe every sensitive listener of the music becomes aware of this. But listening to Arvo's music evokes a sensibility towards something else, and it is this that I should like to explore further. It concerns that dimension of objectivity that, according to what you have said, is achieved through the complementarity of the two voices. When listening, one is aware that we are dealing with a music anchored in a different temporal dimension, removed from the rhythm of conventional linear development. There is something mystical in it all: it is about—I have always had this impression—the mysterium of objectivity.*

But now I would like to return to the chronological sequence of events. If I remember correctly, it was during these years when you were discovering the tintinnabuli style that a very interesting personality appeared, namely Andres Mustonen, with his ensemble Hortus Musicus.

A.P.: When I got to know Mustonen he was a young man of 19, very active and full of energy. He was still a student, and very interested in old music, as I was—so we studied it together. He founded a small vocal group that he directed with great enthusiasm and with which we made a good deal of music together. Sometimes I showed him my sketches, and we considered plans as to how they might be concretely realised. For years I had filled sketch books without even hoping that one day someone could perform them. At that time my music was a music that defied performance. It was not meant for the concert hall and not for any sort of ensemble; it only existed because it was written on the paper, and not even I played it. What sense did it make to play a single line on the piano? Sometimes I invited a musician of the *Hortus*

Musicus to my home and I would ask him to play me some of my melodies on the violin or crumhorn, but that was pitiful, and sounded artificial, particularly with the latter instrument—sounded much too bound to an epoch that had long since past. I tried in vain to hear the sound that I had imagined in the music that was being played. Nonetheless, we attempted some partly polyphonic experiments when I discovered my second voice. And suddenly many works came into being explosively, all at once, all in the year 1977. I would have liked to realise all these works with the musicians of Andres Mustonen, but that was not possible because his ensemble was limited in its instrumentation. Never the less, we were able to realise some of them. What instruments we could count on was rather a matter of chance, so each new experiment was something of an adventure.

E.R.: *Some very illustrious composers, such as Claudio Monteverdi and Johann Sebastian Bach, have found themselves in such precarious conditions, in which they were forced to use whatever instruments were at hand, and to improvise solutions.*

N.P.: Yes, that's true. All these experiences we had to go through allowed Arvo to develop in his new style a sort of connection with the aesthetics of old music—with the epoch in which the real center of a piece of music lay in the pitches, and not in the variety of possible instrumental timbres.

A.P.: One must recognise that in certain situations the timbres of different instruments can contain an element of confusion. One can use the best of things badly. If one uses the internet or a weapon badly, the results can be disastrous. And something like that can happen to an inexperienced composer. Technique can confuse him, and in the end he no longer knows what he's doing. A true master, however, is one who knows the measure for all things.

E.R.: *During all these works and experiments with Mustonen's ensemble, what was your reaction to the discovery of certain passages of old music such as those of the Notre Dame school, for example of a master like Perotinus?*

A.P.: It was wonderful, but that is really another chapter in my life. If I remember correctly we never played music of Perotinus with this ensemble—we would have needed different musicians. But we did play pieces by Guillaume de Machaut, Guillaume Dufay, Jacob Obrecht, Johannes Ockeghem and even of Tomás Luis de Victoria.

E.R.: *Now that you mention Ockeghem, the* Requiem *of this great Flemish composer occurs to me. In view of the epoch and the development of contrapuntal techniques one would expect very complex textures, but exactly the opposite is the case. The most beautiful parts of this mass are written with great simplicity for two voices, and a wonderful sense of innocence reverberates behind the notes. Although I did not know your music when I first heard the two-part sections of Ockeghem's* Requiem *it seemed to me later that this mystic, sublime innocence could be an ideal model for that touching aura that emanates from some passages of your compositions.*

A.P.: As you can see, we are dealing once more with the concept of spirituality. By spirituality I do not mean something mystic, but something in fact quite concrete. There are different attitudes—a very negative way of thinking, and another attitude that sees everything in a positive light. Old music and art teach us to see things from the second of these two perspectives. This is the way Fra Angelico painted, for example, in representing the Day of Judgement. Naturally hell is shown too, but even this seems to be imbued with sanctity, and here hell is simply some "added colour." For other painters that came later, hell was a real place, but heaven was not so pure as that of Fra Angelico.

In this context the words of Peter Brook occur to me: I am thinking of his comments on the legendary Aix-en-Provence production of Don Giovanni. He said that the miracle of Mozart consists in the way he never condemns anyone, how in his works he accompanies his protagonists lovingly and with equal generosity and empathy.

E.R.: *There's a coincidence here that seems truly interesting to me: precisely during those years, at the time of your musical and spiritual experiences in connection with old music, you began to read Dante. But first, can you tell me in which language you read him?*

A.P.: In Russian.

E.R.: *In your opinion were the translations good?*

A.P.: Yes, they were old translations, I think from the 19th century, with a very good commentary. In my opinion Dante found himself in a similar position when he described hell. In his representation of hell one senses a mild light and, instead of harsh judgement, love and sympathy.

E.R.: *I have always found it interesting to follow the reception and exegesis of Dante's poetry in Russia. I still recall my own incredible enthusiasm on reading* Discorso su Dante *by Osip Mandelstam, though today I recognise in his words an interpretation that sees hope as the final outcome of mercy, a hope that the torments of the damned and damnation itself are not eternal, but somehow find redemption in the end. This interpretation, widespread in the Eastern Church, is summed up in the concept of Apokatastase, an interpretation that dissolves in the waves of history and nurtures a sense of compassion towards the world and one's fellow humans, and that radiates in personalities such as Dostoyevski and Gustav Mahler. I have strayed a little from the subject in hand, forgive me, but I am particularly interested in the immanency of Dante's poetry and thought in the contemporary world. Coming back to old music, I'd like to ask you whether you see the Renaissance as belonging to this historic category?*

A.P.: No, for me the Renaissance means something very different than medieval art. It is a time that is imbued with a strong sense of day to day realism.

E.R.: *Does Palestrina belong to the sphere of old music, or already to the Renaissance?*

A.P.: Without a doubt to old music, even if it does lie on the border, and I personally believe that Tomás Luis de Victoria listened to music of the older epoch more than Palestrina. For me, for Mustonen and for most of our musician friends, the centre of Old Music lies with the Ars Nova, the works of Machaut and the Flemish masters, but I remember that we also had many recordings and scores of Josquin.

E.R.: *But between Guillaume de Machaut and Josquin lie several generations.*

A.P.: Yes, but the roots of their thinking, and the goal that their music is aiming toward, is similar.

E.R.: *Does everything then change when, with the Renaissance, we enter the secular polyphony of madrigals?*

A.P.: Yes, musicians slowly began to lose themselves in a sense of the everyday. The world of the Arts became more and more like the people themselves, more realistic, but a very important part was lost. With Andres Mustonen we tried to win back this part that has been lost in modern music, and that is exactly why we dedicated ourselves to old music, getting to know it, playing it.

N.P.: Everything that Arvo has said up to now goes to show how the roots of his style are anchored in Western culture. There has been too much nonsense written about the supposed influence of the chants of the Orthodox Church on his music. Such an influence only became evident later on, and then only in a very limited way.

A.P.: It may be that I am influenced by the tradition of Orthodoxy, but not in the field of music.

E.R.: *The most important influences are in Western polyphony, in the old tradition of Gregorian chant and in the Notre Dame School.*

A.P.: I would like to try to sum it all up with a very simple metaphor. I believe that the thoughts of an innocent child can sometimes be stronger that the superficial complexity of the whole world: a glance from this innocent being can convey a higher truth than anything we can reach with all our ailing endeavours.

E.R.: *Now I'd like to return briefly to a time during the years 1976/77 when so many of your great works were written. Two pieces I particularly admire:* Sarah Was Ninety Years Old, *an extensive work for voices, percussion, and organ, and* Für Alina, *a piece for piano solo that I see as an excellent introduction to this fruitful period of your work.*

A.P.: I wrote *Sarah Was Ninety Years Old* before I had perfected the tintinnabuli style, and it is perhaps my simplest and most abstract work. The piece is purely the result of numerical ratios and restricts itself to the use of four notes. On top of the overall number of 48 possible permutations of these four notes, rhythmic patterns emerge through phase shifting. I emphasise these numerical details because I conceived the whole piece as something that evolves solely on the basis of melodic-rhythmic phases without reaching any tangible result. At the end of the various combinations one can indeed do nothing other than begin all over again and follow exactly the same path as before: the path of Sarah's sterility. The result is always zero, an arid desert, until the angels sent by God appear and everything comes to a close. In the finale of the work a melody arises spontaneously—a sort of lullaby for Isaac. As you see, this is a music based purely on numbers, and I may add that this concentration, this encapsulation within a mathematical formula was something that fascinated me from the beginning, from *Perpetuum Mobile*, which we spoke about earlier, onwards. Anyway, the formula I used in *Sarah Was Ninety Years Old* is connected to a human story and so it was not just a purely theoretical case. *Für Alina*, on the other hand, belongs to the tintinnabuli style, yet it too is structured in a very rational manner. I took the melody randomly from my book of exercises, as if it was a dead melody that meant nothing to me. I constructed a small edifice, a short architectural work from it. I allocated a second melody to this one, following the very simple rules of the tintinnabuli style so that the three notes form a secure tonality in the lower line (b-minor). I had strong doubts as to whether what I had created was really music. I needed time to understand it. On the one hand I knew that my discovery, as I would like to call it, had not arisen by chance, but the composition seemed too simple to me, my ears were not yet used to taking a piece like this seriously. Now I understand that everything was in greater earnest than I could imagine at the time. At that time I was not able to grasp fully the potential possibilities opened up by this sort of composition. I wasn't even sure whether one should read this music horizontally or vertically, was it polyphony or something else? Should I have used more than two melodies? I was tormented by thousands of such doubts, but that did not last very long.

E.R.: *Für Alina was the first essay in an unexplored terrain, reached after a tortuous desert crossing, and in this sense it seems to me fitting to point out how much the numerical dryness upon which* Sarah Was Ninety Years Old *is based explicitly exemplifies this long wait that you spoke of. It is quite understandable that this first work was surrounded by preliminary doubts—albeit doubts that soon evaporated. However, the sheer number of pieces you wrote in so short a time is impressive. The ground you reached proved to be fertile indeed. I am thinking of* Cantus in Memory of Benjamin Britten, Tabula rasa, Missa syllabica. *Could you tell me something about the* Cantus? *That is such a charming work that has been received with great acclaim all over the world, and I was truly touched by the enthusiasm with which Steve Reich spoke of it several times. My first question would be: why* In Memory of Benjamin Britten?

A.P.: The sketches for this piece were already finished when I happened to hear on the radio that Benjamin Britten had died. Some of his pieces were being broadcast on occasion of his death. My wife and I were deeply touched by their tenderness and transparency that evoked the atmosphere of the ballads of Guillaume de Machaut. It was then that my desire to complete my piece and to dedicate it to Britten became concrete. I had wanted to meet and get to know Britten for a long time, but after this news I had to give up the idea for good.

We probably lived in the same house for a while in Armenia, obviously at different times. In the Soviet Union the Composers' Guild had several houses in different places that acted like hotels for composers to work in. I was told that Britten had formerly stayed in the house in Dilijan in Armenia where we were for a time.

E.R.: *You were not lucky enough to meet Britten, but judging from the composition you're talking about, I am sure you feel a great love for his music.*

A.P.: Yes, great love and respect.

N. P. To come back to *Cantus*, we should remember that it was on the 4th of December that we heard the news of Britten's death. This date—and all that happened after it—stayed in our memory for a long time.

A.P.: *Cantus* is simply a proportional canon consisting of a scale. The five different entries are prolonged at each repeat, until all voices coincide: returning 'back home' as in a cadence.

E.R.: *The bare structure of the work alone, as you have just described it, does not explain the enthusiasm that audiences show at every performance.*

A.P.: I think this is due to the transparency and simplicity of the piece's construction, this absolutely clear ordering of the material that we all can perceive, consciously or subconsciously. In my opinion it is to do with vibrations of the instruments that set up a sort of resonance. That is the secret of music, of this sort of music.

E.R.: *I agree, the notes are eloquent, but in order that they may be so, one must structure them in the right manner. But let's now talk about the* Missa syllabica, *a piece that in my opinion plays a central role in your oeuvre.*

A.P.: The *Missa syllabica* is the first composition in which I began to work with a text. I wanted to approach the text not so much with my own emotions and own personal understanding, but rather to use it in an objective way so that one might make use of it in a liturgical context. So I encoded every word, ensuring for example that the final syllable of each word corresponded to the tonic. Of course this generally rather simple mathematical method of construction came from my experience with old music—the musical tradition with which I had meanwhile become very familiar. Now, by referring back to this tradition and to its compositional techniques, I could breathe life into the dead numbers. Those are the simple and Spartan criteria that I followed when setting the *Missa syllabica*. I used various techniques, all on the basis of the text that I worked through word by word in this way. In the *Gloria* I worked with three voices, in *Sanctus* with eight. I have described this purely technical compositional method in detail here, but you shouldn't assume that writing the music just meant following formulae and rules.

E.R.: *I believe that we are dealing once more with the relationship between rules and the exception to the rules. This well known truism that has become somewhat banal through over use needs to be looked at a little more closely. After all, it is the exception that guarantees the usefulness and fertility of the rule. Rigidity in its application masks a very sober attitude to life, and a fundamental inability to recognise the real usefulness of rules.*

A.P.: Yes, we might say that one must be able to alter a rule according to one's intuition.

E.R.: *It seems to me that a compositional process began to take shape with the* Missa syllabica *that was to become a characteristic of your music. I refer to that procedure that grows from the conviction that in a certain way the music is already present in the verses or words that they accompany. The text contains its own music, one only has to entice it out into the open. This attitude is by no means so uncommon: Edgar Varèse saw like this; but what matters is the way in which one tries to entice form from the as yet unformed material. Talking about music that in some way already lies within the spoken word reminds me of Janáček and Mussorgsky. This was the starting point for incredible musical adventures that continued—though sometimes subliminally—to inspire later composers to whom such ideas might appear foreign. This need not surprise us perhaps, when one thinks of the relationship between Mussorgsky, Ravel, and Poulenc, between Janáček and Steve Reich.*

A.P.: One might find other interesting parallels in the music of Salvatore Sciarrino, whose work is full of extraordinary discoveries. I don't know how he went about it, but I can say that in my work I take account of the number of syllables, commas, full stops, and accents. From time to time it may happen that I unconsciously feel a closer affiliation to particular words, but that is not the main factor. I try to keep a certain distance from the text, and ideally I manage to view it from an angle which allows me to imagine a purely objective psalm recitation echoing around a church, growing out of a single note. This would indeed be the echo of an international language.

E.R.: *Like a bas-relief.*

A.P.: Yes, absolutely.

E.R.: *On hearing* Missa syllabica *and* Passio *I somehow intuitively sensed what we have said up to now on this subject—that will hardly surprise you. I recognised a special dimension in these works that I interpreted as a challenge to the listener to believe in the objective reality of numbers, since these are—especially in their essential independence from the subject—closest to transcendence. To be honest I should add that I first had this experience many years ago when I heard the Latin works of Stravinsky. A long time later I learnt of something Stravinsky said, namely how much satisfaction he gained from dealing with the Latin language, since it seemed to him that through this language implicit meaning was more easily grasped, without drifting off into psychological deliberation. Seldom have I shared an opinion so utterly; that is why I'm also so interested in the relationship you develop towards the text. In dealing with language, we tend to show our own state of mind and forget that words possess a clear, precise meaning that inclines to be overshadowed by emotions. All too often we abuse language, whereas we should treat it with the utmost care. When you approach a text you pay great attention to the scansion of syllables and to punctuation. That seems to me an important lesson.*

N.P.: One should bear in mind here that there is a precisely-formulated tradition. The liturgical texts should be read syllable by syllable, full stop by full stop, comma by comma. Tradition demands that the comma has the same weight as the word. Perhaps we sometimes forget it, but in the Gospels, too, each word has equal weight.

A.P.: And that should be audible in the concert hall.

E.R.: *Yes, but on stage it can happen that a singer will have a beautiful voice but poor diction, which distorts the sound of the words in a ridiculous way.*

But now I'd like you to tell me something about Arbos, *one of your purely instrumental works.*

A.P.: This is again a proportional canon in three parts: the first part represents the trunk of an imaginary tree, then comes the second voice, twice as fast as the first, then the third, twice as fast as the second. Everything is organised rhythmically in a simple way, interrupted by rests. It is pure mathematics—mathematics applied to musical instruments. That sounds odd, doesn't it? But in music everything is mathematics, without numbers there wouldn't be a single note.

E.R.: *We might also add that the numbers become time, since, when we talk of different tempos, it is numbers that regulate their progression. In my opinion one of the key concepts of your music lies in exactly this simultaneity of many tempos. In* Passio *for example Jesus Christus has a very particular tempo that is half as fast as the surrounding context, and I believe that in comparison to the tempos of the other figures—Pilatus, the Evangelists, the crowd—the tempo of Jesus embodies eternity, its slowness is for me symbolic. Generally in this work there is clearly a recognisable, well-calculated dramatic structuring of the temporal dimension.*

Sometimes a single moment in your music is extended as if it would lift the temporal dimension from its hinges.

N.P.: I could quote several examples of this. The last chord in *Cantus* seems not to want to come to an end. It stands still, without growing or diminishing. Something has been achieved and now one doesn't want to let it go. The content of the entire work strives towards this point. When the plateau of this cadence has been reached the chord does not want to stop. The same thing happens at the end of the first part of *Tabula rasa*: always this final chord that appears to want to go on for ever.

E.R.: *I have noticed that this technique has consolidated from work to work. In the* Missa syllabica *you experimented with it for the first time, but in the works that followed the temporal introspection of the text has increasingly deepened and allows an intense dramaturgy of tempos and registers to come into play.*

Thinking along these lines, we might approach the Passio *and examine the importance of the role of punctuation.*

A.P.: Everything to do with punctuation is just in the instrumental parts. All the rest belongs to the realm of the voices, even when they are accompanied.

E.R.: *Forgive my interrupting, but how did you arrive at the idea of writing a Passion in the first place?*

A.P.: I sketched out the entire work in a few days.

N.P.: In fact it was more than two days. We were in Tallinn at the beginning of Lent. He said, "During Lent this year I want to write a Passion." So he started to work without setting himself definite goals and without any particular objective and he continued without stopping till the end.

A.P.: It was partly a version with a single voice. The second was simply a mirrored voice, running parallel to the first.

N.P.: After that we moved to the West, and Alfred Schlee from Universal Edition managed to arrange a commission for Arvo from Bavarian Radio. Arvo took the existing work back in hand and rewrote it, much more finely-worked. He says two days, because he already had the basic structure of the work he conceived in Estonia, complete, in his head. But I do remember how the work took on its final form. In our flat in Berlin we had hung up a piece of blue cloth about five or six metres long on one wall onto which we stuck coloured sheets of paper with the various texts of the Passion. Each figure had its own colour so that Arvo could take in the whole thing at a glance. The whole structure of the work was like a picture. Incidentally, Arvo did the same thing with other large works in order to get a visual picture. He had to feel the entire musical progression and to take it in all at once, to force the entire 75 minutes of the Passion into a fraction of that time. I think we're touching upon one of the most interesting phenomena of the tintinnabuli style here: the way it can overcome the barrier of time.

A.P.: If you look at this long cloth from a particular angle, it acts like a chord.

E.R.: *You have said that your final reason for leaving Tallinn was the decision to emigrate to the West. Do you also remember how you came to make this decision?*

A.P.: A lot of things were going on then, but it was the behaviour of the government people towards me that was the decisive factor. They made it quite clear to me that they would "not be displeased" if my wife and I were to leave the country. I had practically no chance of surviving as a composer because the functionaries I depended on for my existence acted towards me with constant animosity. In their opinion performances of my works abroad had become too frequent, but since the première of a composition without the composer being present was seen as a scandal, they felt obliged to let me go. The critics that reviewed my works in the West were positive, but that just led to a worsening of my position, which in a short time became unbearable both for them and for me.

E.R.: *Sofia Gubaidulina, Alfred Schnittke, and Edison Denisov told me the same thing. Success in the West meant animosity and persecution in the Soviet Union. This was the revenge of mediocre composers who were usually eager party servants, well able to fit in to the invisible but indestructible organogram that ordered the flow of grants and well-paid commissions. I was shocked by the grotesque farce of performances of works by these so ideologically-praiseworthy composers: whole companies of soldiers were recruited to fill up the concert halls, and afterwards everyone spoke of a work's huge success and its resonance with the public! And it is well known with what satisfaction this same pack of mediocre composers doggedly criticised the influence of Prokofiev and Shostakovich in the years before Stalin's death. To describe this pitiful scenario would require the satirical wit of a Nikolai Gogol, a wit so keenly honed in his novel* Dead Souls. *But let's get back to your emigration. What did you feel, you and your family, when you boarded the train to leave your hometown for ever?*

A.P.: It was a journey into the unknown. There was myself, my wife, two children, and I believe nine suitcases. Until we reached Brest we were accompanied by my wife's aunt and Toomas Siitan, a student at the Conservatory, who helped us (he is now a Professor at the Music Academy in Tallinn).

N.P.: I'd like to take a small step back to recall some other details. In Moscow a musician like Arvo would have had to reckon with more serious consequences for his behaviour. In Estonia the official functionaries acted in a rather more confused manner. They asked themselves: who was responsible for this escalation of the conflict with Arvo Pärt? They quarrelled amongst themselves and in the end they no longer knew how they should behave towards him.

A.P.: I'd like to add a small detail: when I began to write using twelve-tone technique, functionaries and other composers were really irritated by it, but then they themselves started to use this technique. Ten years later, after I had already given up twelve-tone technique and had developed in quite a new direction, these same composers, who by now thoroughly believed in the method, thought that I had gone mad and found it all absurd.

E.R.: *If I am not mistaken, it was suggested to you that you should emigrate. Who made this suggestion?*

N.P.: In autumn a leading member of the Central Committee visited us at home and recommended that we leave the country. It was meant to look like a voluntary decision, but in reality it was an eviction order from the state and was at that time irreversible.

This sort of "polite" behaviour was convenient for those in power, and the public could stamp us as traitors. After this visit we immediately began to prepare the documents for our expatriation, because staying was impossible. Shortly afterwards Arvo was advised to leave the Guild of Composers. Quite by chance some colleagues gathered in the corridor, members of the committee of the Composers Guild, to give Arvo "friendly" advice: that he should leave the Guild voluntarily. Dramatic events at that time happened in this unspectacular and prosaic way—without meetings or protocols. That was the way the system worked: by covering up the real facts. And with these tactics the system achieved truly "remarkable" results. What actually happened— that is to say the deportation—was covered up, both in Estonia and in the West. Some recently published articles that "document" the allegedly "good life" of Arvo Pärt in Estonia prove this. In this way the Soviet machinery of disinformation was efficiently transferred to the West and it is practically impossible to eradicate the misinformation it spreads. When Arvo came back home that day from the Composers' Guild he was paler than I have ever seen him. For the first time I began to worry whether he would ever get over leaving his home country. It took two or three weeks for us to organise our departure and to clear out the flat—for which there was already a long waiting list of interested people. We just didn't know where we could go, but we had no intention at all of going to Israel, the only country for which we'd been granted an exit visa. In the hurry and excitement we left some scores behind and I can't remember any longer to whom we entrusted them. In or-der to export a manuscript one needed the permission of the Department of Culture in the form of a rectangular stamp. To make doubly sure that the most important manuscripts would be allowed through, an employee of the Department of Culture, in a well meaning gesture, added a second stamp— this time a round one—to the first. But when we reached the border we were told that precisely this round stamp was never allowed to leave the Soviet Union because it was interpreted as signifying a state secret. Luckily they did let us across the border with our things. There was no time for nostalgia or emotions, we had to leave. All our friends came to us in the flat and Andres Mustonen came with his whole orchestra. Then we opened all the doors and the whole stairwell was full of music and tears. I remember a large strong man who cried a lot when he said goodbye, and there was no hope of a re-union. One of my aunts came from Georgia to help us pack. She also helped us financially because we didn't have enough money to embark on such a journey, and we also had to pay a large sum of money for the expatriation— almost to buy our freedom. My aunt accompanied us to the train and gave me a ring and a couple of wooden spoons—though I wasn't allowed to keep these, because it was forbidden to export things like that.

At five o'clock in the morning we got into two taxis in Tallinn and we said to our children that we were embarking on a journey round the world, and that at the end of such journeys you always had to come back to where you started. One person came to the Baltic Station in Tallinn to say goodbye: the musicologist Helju Tauk. A remarkable event occurred at the border station of Brest-Litovsk at the customs control. When we arrived with our children and small amount of luggage the customs officer asked us, "Where is your luggage? Is that all?" The other people waiting at the station were heavily laden with luggage of all kinds, they even had furniture and someone even had a piano. We just had a few suitcases and even these were half empty! But we still had to open them and so the cassettes with the recordings of Arvo's first works appeared. Then one customs officer said, "Oh, you are musicians. I also played in Estonia." Straight away they wanted to check the cassettes with our tape-recorder and so we heard *Missa syllabica*, then *Arbos*, and then even *Cantus*. The station hall was a gigantic building with a domed roof as high as a church and we were inside this huge place alone with the border police. There I could really feel the effect that music had on people: suddenly everything was so relaxed, so normal, so beautiful. Our Michael lay in the cradle, a friend had knitted a new coat and all the women border police tried to copy the pattern. A police woman led us into a room where they undressed Michael to check whether we had perhaps hidden something in the clothes in which he was wrapped. From all the icons that we had at home we had taken just one, so small that we could hide it in one of Michael's pockets. They didn't find it. Michael started to cry and the policeman let us bring him some biscuits. It was an unforgettable scene—not least because everything was accompanied by Arvo's music. Everything turned out alright, and after a short time we got onto the train to Vienna. We knew that the emigrants were to be brought together in a camp there, where they would wait for their outward journey to Israel.

A.P.: Or Rome.

N.P.: Yes, in Rome there was a sort of distribution centre for the emigrants who wanted to go to America, I believe. The situation was difficult at any rate, because until then we had no contact with the outside world. And we didn't know what was going to happen to us. At this point something unexpected occurred. I think it was Alfred Schnittke who had somehow let

Universal Edition in Vienna know that Arvo Pärt was coming to Vienna with all the emigrants going to Israel. The fact is that on Sunday, the 20ᵗʰ of January, 1980, at 7 o'clock in the morning, a woman who had been sent by the publisher was at the station in Vienna and called out loudly: "Where is Arvo Pärt? Herr Pärt, please come to me immediately!" If this woman had not been there waiting for us we should have landed with all the rest in the collection centre. This woman was called Elena Hift and she said that the publisher could help us to get Austrian citizenship if we would "work" for Universal Edition. We didn't know what we should do, we were too confused to understand what it meant to have the prospect of obtaining a Western citizenship. So Elena Hift accompanied us to a guest house where she had reserved rooms for us. The week before Neeme Järvi had left Tallinn, and by chance had lived in just this guest house. That was how Arvo's work for Universal Edition started.

E.R.: *So then you lived in Vienna for quite a time.*

N.P.: No, just a year and a half. Alfred Schlee, the director of the publisher, took it upon himself to contact the DAAD[10] to suggest us for a grant—something we couldn't have done on our own. And this grant then arrived after one and a half years, after we had received Austrian citizenship.

E.R.: *Are you still Austrian citizens?*

N.P.: Yes, of course.

E.R.: *So you live in Berlin, but are Austrian citizens, and your children too.*[11]

A.P.: Yes, that's true. That is exactly what happened to György Ligeti.

---

10   The abbreviation DAAD stands for Deutscher Akademischer Austauschdienst. This is a valuable German institution that awards grants to foreign teachers, researchers, and artists for lengthy terms of study or professional activity.
11   Arvo and Nora Pärt moved back to Estonia, where they posess dual citizenship, in 2010.

E.R.: *That's right, there are many parallels between your past and his. He also lived for a while in Vienna before moving to Hamburg. Your story is very moving, and I'd like to thank you for having told it in such a personal and trusting way.*

Just a few years later, in 1982, the première of the Passio *took place in Munich. I assume that it was a great success; in any case the CD recording of this composition helped it become internationally known a few years later.*

N.P.: In fact the Munich performance was not a success, there were lots of bad critiques. The choir of the Bavarian Radio did their best, and finally a performance emerged that was really not too bad, but it wasn't really the *Passio*. For many years Arvo was unconvinced of the quality of the composition, and only changed his mind after hearing the interpretation of the Hilliard Ensemble.

E.R.: *When was the CD recorded?*

A.P.: Much later, in 1988 I believe.

N.P.: The same thing happened with the *Te Deum*: not until seven years after the première was it sung in an interpretation that Arvo liked.

E.R.: *It doesn't surprise me that a contemporary work first finds real acceptance with the public through a recording. That is typical of the culture of our time— one could cite many examples. I, too, am one of those who succumbed to the fascination of this recording.*

A.P.: The première on the other hand was itself of no great importance and took place in front of a very sparse audience in the church.

E.R.: *To what church are you referring?*

A.P.: The Lukaskirche on the Marienplatz in Munich. The audience wasn't used to hearing so many rests, and that made it difficult for them to follow the logic of the work. The singers also had a certain amount of trouble with the very large vocal leaps over the course of more than an hour. After this première I revised the lengths of the rests, and I am actually not happy about this, since perhaps something of the original idea has been lost. With the Hilliard Ensemble the intonation was exemplary: this work demands perfect intonation. The same thing happened again with *De Profundis*, with *Cantate Domino,* and with *An den Wassern zu Babel (By the waters of Babylon)*. Only then did I become aware that I had made the right choice with my compositional technique, and I understood that this type of music was really viable.

E.R.: *How did your first meeting with the Hilliard Ensemble come about?*

A.P.: I believe Paul Hillier had heard some of my music, possibly an old recording with Andres Mustonen in Tallinn. So he decided to contact me and I went to London to meet him.

E.R.: *Was this your first trip to London?*

A.P.: No, I had been there before I moved from Tallinn, to the première of *Cantus* in the Royal Albert Hall. Much later I returned several times and I worked together with Paul for the first time on a recording of some of my works at the BBC. Another opportunity arose with the Almeida Festival, where many of my works were performed.

E.R.: *Paul Hillier was deeply moved by your music from the start and so he decided to work on some of your pieces with his ensemble.*

A.P.: Exactly.

N.P.: I remember that we were speechless when we heard those rehearsals for the BBC recording. They sang with absolute perfection, and the organist Christopher Bowers-Broadbent was wonderful too, and showed enormous sensitivity to the style of Arvo's music in his choice of registers.

A.P.: We had never heard such pure fifths and thirds.

N.P.: Everything was perfect, intonation, phrasing, everything was sung with just the right tone colour. I can remember that after he heard them Arvo said, "I have nothing to add. It is all perfect." We were moved to tears, overjoyed to have found people that were suited to this music in every way. When one thinks of all the difficulties we encountered elsewhere in getting Arvo's new way of thinking across to musicians, helping them to find the right sound. For interpreters of his music it was like recovering from culture shock.

A.P.: I don't know if the CD with *Tabula rasa* was already available at that time.

N.P.: I'm not sure either, but I believe Manfred Eicher,[12] the producer at ECM was present at the BBC recording.

E.R.: *In any case, this CD was a wonderful way of propagating your music.*

N.P.: There had been some destructive reactions from critics to performances of *Tabula rasa*, and they didn't stop until the recording—then still on LP. The situation did change after it appeared, though the rejection did still continue from some quarters.

E.R.: *If I am not mistaken, Gidon Kremer performed a new version of* Fratres *at the Salzburg Festival.*

N.P.: Yes, and this event was also organised by Alfred Schlee. But experience had taught us that, although one can have a great concert performance that generates genuine enthusiasm, real public resonance comes only with optimal recordings.

E.R.: *When did you meet Manfred Eicher for the first time?*

A.P.: He told us himself that quite by chance, during a car ride, he heard a piece of mine that impressed him deeply. It was *Tabula rasa* in a recording

---

12 Manfred Eicher is founder and producer of the legendary recording label ECM, under which the most important works of Arvo Pärt have appeared.

made for West German Radio in Cologne. Manfred stopped the car to listen to the piece to the end and straight afterwards he began trying to find out about this music and its author. He later contacted Gidon Kremer and Dennis Russell Davies and produced a recording of *Fratres*. He added *Cantus* and the recording of *Tabula rasa* that he had heard during the car journey in order to fill the CD.

Eicher always worked in an exemplary manner. He spent much time and energy in engaging good musicians. It was very important to him to arrange pieces on a CD in a dramatically skilful way, which turned the CD into a work of art in itself. Another typical feature of this recording label is that old recordings stay in its catalogue. As you know, with large recording labels recordings remain available for a few years and then are removed from the catalogue. The recording of the *Passio* is an example of his way of working. We performed it with the Hilliard Ensemble at least twenty or thirty times before we recorded it. As you probably know, the way even the best orchestras work is quite different. A new piece is read a few times at sight and then is recorded directly. If you are lucky the conductor suggests recording a second version.

N.P.: I'd like to illustrate how we made recordings with ECM with an example from *Miserere*. In the middle of the *Miserere* the choir enters with the *Dies irae*. This is a very tricky moment for the recording from the point of view of the dynamics because it is acoustically quite different from the rest of the piece. If you sit in a church and listen it all sounds fantastic, then you listen to the same thing through loudspeakers in a studio—and the sound is very poor. So we spent two whole days resetting microphones and changing their position until after long discussions all through the night we managed to get to grips with the problem. With a different recording company we would never have had the opportunity of searching for such a long time for just the right sound.

E.R.: *A final question about* Passio. *What is the relationship between the instrumental quartet and the vocal quartet? Why did you use exactly this instrumentation—oboe, bassoon, violin, and cello?*

A.P.: These four instruments—along with the organ that accompanies Pilatus, the *turba* choirs, and Jesus—allowed me to create a broad palette of sound. With the help of the four instruments I could build up an eight-part texture in sections of the Gospel, in which continual changes in timbre follow one another, resulting in all possible combinations of the various voices and instruments, until a sort of acoustic rhombus or compact plateau of sound appears which then gradually dissolves. The construction of this wave takes up about a quarter of the whole composition.[13] During the course of the work there are sections with Pilatus, the *turba* choirs, and Jesus that have their own internal logic, but the overall structure is conceived and realised as I have described. I would like to add that the various facets—also of timbre—that occur as a result of the variety of persons involved in a particular scene, are already laid down in the Gospel, and that the dramatic structure is already there in the libretto. I didn't use any psalm or any other material, I took everything as it was written. To begin with I was very confused, it seemed as if nothing would sound as good as I had hoped, and this rather idiosyncratic combination of instruments didn't entirely convince me. Then I realised that I had first to become accustomed to this unusual sound world and when I had done that it all seemed to flow in a much more linear manner. The rehearsals, at first slow and strenuous, became more fluent. *Tabula rasa* is for example a piece that could be played by semi-professional musicians, but in the early days not even great interpreters could master it.

N.P.: One day Gidon Kremer came to Tallinn and asked Arvo to write a piece for him.

A.P.: Yes, I can remember. He said he was going to perform a piece of Schnittke in a concert in Tallinn and that he would like me to write a piece for the same

---

13   Arvo Pärt is referring to the process of progressively building up layers in the vocal and instrumental sections—a process that should be understood in relation to the structure of the text of the Evangelist. This consists of 210 phrases that Pärt subdivides into four sections, each consisting of 50 phrases, and a closing group of 10 phrases. Each of the four sections begins with a different solo voice that sings two phrases (not forgetting that the part of the Evangelist is given to a vocal quartet—soprano, counter tenor, tenor, baritone, thus allowing for the possibility of colouring the various entries of the Evangelist in a variety of ways). Thus all phrases undergo a change of texture and tone colour. The other voices and instruments follow the opening solo voice one by one, until a maximum density of eight voices is reached. At this point the process of subtraction begins, with a texture that slowly dissolves until just the solo voices are left. This process is repeated in a sequence of arches.

instrumentation. I limited myself to asking him whether he would be prepared to play very slow music, and he answered that he had no problem with that.

N.P.: So Arvo wrote the piece and Gidon Kremer and Tatjana Gridenko received the manuscript of *Tabula rasa*. At the first rehearsal they didn't have the faintest idea how the piece should be played, but it got worse when the rehearsals with the orchestra started. Gidon must have thought that he had landed himself a huge problem in asking for the piece! The conductor Eri Klas applied himself to the task and Schnittke tried to save what there was to be saved at the piano. He even went so far as to suggest that the members of the orchestra be placed differently on the stage, but even that didn't work. After two or three rehearsals the musicians shut away their instruments in their cases and said to us, "We can do no more." A few hours later at the concert we all arrived pale with shock, imagining a catastrophe to be looming on the horizon. Gidon was very nervous, but when they began to play, miraculously everything went perfectly. I have never since heard such a stillness as the silence in the hall at the end of the work.

A.P.: The silence was so intoxicating that the people were almost afraid to breathe!

E.R.: *You said that during the period in which you were trying to develop a new way of hearing you were reluctant to listen to any other sort of music. It seems to me that the attempt was completely successful, judging by the* scepsis *with which you seem to view conventional instrumentation in your handling of the unusual accompanying parts that interweave with the part of the Evangelist. In addition to new instrumental sound colour I'd like to look more closely at an inherent paradox in your works: on the one hand you are interested in conquering new acoustic horizons, on the other hand you are steeped in an ancient and eloquent tradition. Primarily your compositions belong to the genre of sacred music. We have mentioned* Missa syllabica *and the* Passio, *but the list could go on with the* Te Deum, *the* Stabat Mater, *the* Miserere. *But before we talk about these pieces I would like to learn how you experience your own affinity to musical tradition, since behind each of these works lies an impressive history.*

A.P.: I have always allowed myself to be guided by texts that mean a lot to me and that for me are of existential significance. It is a root that reaches very deep and that lifts me upwards. It is basically the same fruit that has nourished the world for centuries. If we view a period of two thousand years we recognise that people have changed very little. That is why I believe the sacred texts are still "contemporary." Seen in this light there are no significant differences between yesterday, today, and tomorrow because there are truths that maintain their validity. Mankind feels much the same today as he did then and has the same need to free himself from his faults. The texts exist independently of us and are waiting for us: each of us has a time when he will find a way to them. This meeting happens when the texts are not treated as literature or works of art but as points of reference, or as models. "Everything has its time," says Solomon, and indeed "there is a time to laugh and a time to cry." Our conscience and our intellect are the scales in which our decisions are weighed: we were given the freedom of choice and no one other than God can allow themselves to judge, because only He knows the nature of time. Everything that I have said to you here is directly connected with my compositions, including those that you have just named.

E.R.: *You have just clarified an important point with regard to your texts. According to how they are treated they can be seen as literature, art, or as a model. These are very different categories, and in this desire to distinguish between different ways of looking at the same text perhaps the answer lies. When I spoke of traditions that have accrued around these texts, I was referring to a large number of works that are really works of art.*

A.P.: Of course the texts of my works can be treated in this manner, but one shouldn't do that. When we take the *Stabat Mater* we recognise that it is a poem, the *Psalms of David* are also poetry, but these texts are not just poetry. They are part of the Holy Scripture. They are both at once, and we must choose which door we want to go through to reach the treasure. Just as they are bound to universal truths, so do they touch upon intimate truths, purity, beauty, that ideal core to which each human being is bound! This core has extraordinary power and warmth, it is like a solar system where everything is interconnected. Of course everyone has their own particular path to follow on this earth, and it is possible that simpler people have a more direct vision and feel this nearness more strongly, just as more cultivated people may experience greater difficulty in grasping this kind of connection. But perhaps I've said too much!

E.R.: *Not at all, I am very glad to hear you speak with such honesty of these profound matters that touch upon much that I hold most dear in life, things that acquire a new, heightened intimacy just as they seem to distance themselves from culture. I couldn't say whether it is good or bad, but the fact is that cultural identification in people who have had a long intellectual schooling in the end tends to resemble a conditioned reflex. We don't notice it, but we are prisoners of an unavoidable system of references that, in effect, "genetically" alters our intellectual life. When I read the text of the* Stabat mater *I hear the music of Pergolesi and other composers who have set these words and I find myself drifting in a sea of iconographic points of reference, all with their own colours, gestures, and luminosity. Perhaps it is pointless to hold a grudge against one's memory, which, in hoarding everything, hinders us from regaining any innocence—and yet we cannot suppress that desire which would lead us back to the untouched nature of things. However, you seem to think that this is genuinely possible, since, according to what you have just said, this flood of memories, so difficult to keep in check, is a distraction that diverts us from the true nature of the text. Accordingly, the musical shadows of Pergolesi, Bach, and Vivaldi are shields that with their beauty distract us from the true nature of the text.*

A.P.: I don't think that all that is a problem. All those you mentioned are better composers than I am!

N.P.: One mustn't ignore the fact that Arvo, when he wrote his *Stabat mater,* had emancipated himself from Pergolesi and the other composers, as he did from everything that represents tradition.

E.R.: *I think I gathered that when you told us that Arvo for several years made an intense effort to develop a new kind of hearing: that indeed implies freeing oneself from tradition, because, as wonderful as it may be, it can also block our creativity.*

A.P.: You see, perhaps I was following a tradition other than the musical tradition—we shouldn't forget that there are very many paths that run parallel to music. The differences that we notice in the way various composers treat the texts represent a tradition in itself—like a railway station with tracks fanning out in different directions. One must bear in mind that each epoch expresses its own needs.

E.R.: *I asked a very simple question from which a wealth of far-reaching observations have sprung. However, I would like to stay with this subject for a while and ask whether you find this affinity to the sacred, so predominant in your music, can be a limitation as well.*

A.P.: Absolutely not, in fact quite the opposite. I would like to say that only time will tell what will happen and what will last, we cannot know that ourselves. In Gregorian chant, in the works of some great composers and in folk music the same thing happened. A composer cannot for example decide to write a song that will last for five hundred years in the folk music tradition, in the end it is the people who decide what lasts. As you can see it is an absolutely objective process, that also holds true for the field of sacred music. I cannot believe, as some of the critics do however, that I belong to a category of *"sacred minimalism."* This subject is really not worth talking about.

N.P.: From the perspective of the liturgical music tradition, the music that Arvo writes can be seen as being completely secular.

A.P.: It seems to me that this is a relative matter. I have no intention at all of writing secular music, but I am not in a position to be able to write sacred music either.

E.R.: *How do you explain the success of your music? You have just said that only the test of time counts. In fact for several years your compositions have been extremely successful.*

A.P.: It is possible that the people who follow my music with interest hope to find something in it. Or perhaps these are people who, like me, are in search of something and when listening to my music feel that it is moving in the same direction as they are.

N.P.: I believe that Arvo's music is more directed towards the ear than to the intellect. And we shouldn't forget that this culture, this ability to listen in an unprejudiced way, has almost completely disappeared from the world of contemporary music. One can listen to music with a wealth of different expectations, one can look for particular interpretations, technical effects, and new musical ideas. All these expectations are valid but one should still be in a position simply to give oneself up to sound itself, something that particularly for musicians has become a problem. I believe that this is the cause of the distaste that some musicians feel for Arvo's music. Confronted with his music they tackle it intellectually, and on hearing the first note they think, "Oh, we know that already," but in fact they have not really listened to the music at all. And yet this music should really teach one how to hear in the first place—if only one can trust it.

A.P.: On top of this, I work with simple numbers that are easy to see and to hear, I look for a common denominator. I strive for a music that I might call universal, in which many dialects are blended together.

N.P.: In any case for Arvo is it first and foremost the desire to reach music's roots that counts: the basic cell, so to speak, this deep root that can produce such varied fruits, and that is why so many different people recognise themselves within it.

A.P.: I believe that one should accept the fact that people in our epoch feel the need to breathe out, and not just to breathe in. We need a way of thinking that is free of conflict.

N.P.: Yes, but that is a dangerous definition, because *New Age* is also striving for a conflict-free way of making music. Arvo's music is, however, not a soothing music, it also contains pain and pity. I believe that is an important characteristic of Arvo's musical language and also the big difference to *New Age* music.

E.R.: *I must admit that I wouldn't have thought of New Age but I would like to try to add a further observation to the debate about your music. Let us assume that people enjoy listening to tonal music. If, however, you suggest to these people that they should listen to neo-tonal music, of the kind that certain neo-romantic composers have tried in vain to establish, then it just doesn't work. Audiences reject this music, in spite of the fact that it traces the codes of tonal music. People like listening to your music on the other hand—often with great dedication—although it can only in a very broad sense be defined as tonal music, since it makes no use of the structural relationships of harmony upon which tonal music is based. It is therefore possible—yes, even probable—that people feel themselves drawn to your music because they perceive a new and at the same time encouraging signal. The acoustic data is immediately recognisable—the triads of the tintinnabuli style leave no doubt about that—but they are not rigidly frozen in a convention. It is as if we were being invited to see an old bas-relief in another light that allows us to recognise other meanings, other vibrations. Because the acoustic material in which these musical events are chiselled appears miraculously fresh and vibrating, like a living being.*

A.P.: When a person looks at a work of art, a building, or something new, it is as if his eyes are opened again, aroused by a new stimulus. In music the same thing happens with the ear. We immediately try to grasp the internal logic—how a musical structure is built, what rules hold it together. I believe that this also happens with my tintinnabuli style. It is something new that is also felt to be something foreign and "other," but not something absurd. The fact that the unusual aspect is more or less obvious is also due to the way it is realised musically. But this has nothing to do with originality at any price. A logical structure can work as a foundation when it is based on simple, comprehensible concepts. If things become exaggeratedly complicated, as if often the case with much contemporary music, people can no longer follow the musical thoughts of the composer and they don't even grasp the important innovations in the sound-world of the composition.

This sort of music is often difficult to listen to and to understand—and I am not talking here about harder or softer musical languages, but I refer simply to the functional technical structuring of the piece, whose

construction should be perceivable. It doesn't need to be all so complicated! A good writer considers the first sentence of each of his books very
carefully, because he knows very well that it all depends on this sentence,
whether the reader will carry on reading or close the book. What I mean
is that one should be able to move within clearly outlined borders of comprehensibility. A composer should use this rule as a starting point for his
own work, in other words he should be in a position to understand what
he is doing at any given moment. I know enough composers who come
to the first rehearsal of their new piece without the least idea of how it
should sound.

N.P.: The real problem of contemporary music lies in the difficulty of com-
munication: each composer creates his own personal language without there
being any possibility of a translation, and the result is that composers write
books about the language themselves. How many words we read in programme leaflets! And these are really words that are basically trying to com-
pensate for the deficit that arises in the listener's perception of the music.
The result is that everyone speaks his own language, a language that only
makes sense for one single individual.

A.P.: And very often the explanation has very little to do with the sound
itself.

N.P.: Many composers complain that their time has not yet come and at some
time in the future everything will be different. In a way they are right, because our ears really do accustom themselves to new impulses very slowly,
but that isn't the only aspect of the problem.

E.R.: *I have no doubt of the broad comprehensibility of Arvo's music, and I am
aware of its remarkable ability to arouse interest in the most varied of audiences. However, I would like to say that understanding is a terribly complicated
business. What does understanding music mean? How many types and layers of
understanding are there? Is it legitimate to sneer at other sorts of understanding
that are different from our own? Trying to understand music in order to explain
it to other people—I have made this my profession, but over the years I have*

developed an increasing respect for other people's ways of understanding. I don't mean by this that I place the listening habits and the intellect of others above all else: I know very well that one can find oneself on a slippery path that would lead to a Proustian praise of Bad Music. What I would like to emphasise is rather the trust in music, trust in its ability gradually to find a place for itself in people's understanding. When I consider the fascination that Arvo's music arouses in other people, the picture of a misty dawn amidst meadows and mountains occurs to me. Hundreds of people stood or squatted in the grass to listen to a choir that was singing a new piece of Arvo's. That so many people were taking part—people who had gotten up at five o'clock in the morning and gone off walking to hear music that at dawn would echo all around the mountains[14]—this says something about the need for spirituality, or that the world today has, in your own words, the aching need to follow alternative paths. The seductive power of your music reminds me of that of Steve Reich. He is American, you are Estonian, you have different cultural roots, but nonetheless you both have a common language that brings sounds to new life by suspending the structural functions of harmony.

A.P.: Yes, that's right. And Reich is always on the lookout for something new, in each work he is very creative.

E.R.: *With his speech melody at the end of the 1980's he succeeded in impressing a particular memorability upon spoken vocal parts that brings everyday experience into music. I am thinking of* Different Trains *for string quartet and tape recorder with which he managed to conquer even the most condescending of listeners.*

A.P.: There were amazingly clever solutions in *The Cave* as well. I remember all that he managed to get out of the word *Abraham*.

E.R.: *We have spoken of the great success that your music has enjoyed with the public. Now I would like to talk in more detail about the critical reception of your work. How have you faired with music critics and musicologists?*

---

14   In the summer of 2003 the festival *Klänge der Dolomiten* put on a concert series dedicated to the music of Arvo Pärt. One of the concerts took place at sunrise in the open air.

A.P.: Above all we must respect that there are many ways of looking at things, as you just said, and I believe that according to their own particular perspective all these ways are valid. But it can happen that critics succumb to prejudice or are simply unaccustomed to a certain kind of music. Of course one enjoys reading a professional, well-meaning critique, who can deny that. But a bad critique, even if it is unfounded, tendentious, and painful to read can be of greater use, and is refreshing.

One must take critics seriously, but not too seriously. One should make an effort to see them like any other human being, because deep down none of us knows the ultimate truth, or knows exactly what is right or wrong, and what effect a work will have in the course of time. But perhaps it would be better if Nora were to speak about these things.

N.P.: When we came to the West, Arvo was a real gift for the media. It was such a gratifying topic to report about: an exotic being, mystic, monk, beard, medieval vocabulary, detached from the world, etc. It wasn't all meant in a bad way (though some was bad enough) and the more well-meaning it was the more the distorted picture upset us and did us harm. The idea that within the field of spirituality there can also exist a normality and naturalness that doesn't land immediately in the realms of mysticism was obviously quite foreign to the general public.

A.P.: Some people even thought I wore a false beard!

N.P.: At first Arvo was too careless and ingenuous. He completely trusted the media with his honest and naïve way of explaining things. These same explanations were used against him in a very hurtful way, so that he could never use them again. In some way we were ourselves responsible for these unexpected distortions.

A.P.: Yes, l when I speak openly about my ideals it can happen that my own words are turned against me.

N.P.: We had to swallow many banal and insulting accusations—but we shouldn't talk about that here, they were more personal insults than critiques. If a person is raised up very high it is as if a bubble forms around him that sooner or later must burst. Sometimes a critic can praise you to the sky, then a little later the same critic can no longer stand his own exaggeration and he drags you roughly back down to earth. It is like the natural law of equilibrium that cannot abide a state of imbalance and tries to bring everything back into balance.

A.P.: However, it is only some of the critics who express themselves so carelessly, perhaps because there is as yet no critical tradition for the reception of my music. Some beginnings have been made regarding my tintinnabuli style, and these shed a little light in the general fog, but one must bear in mind that while my music has already found a place with the audience, the theoretical side that should go hand in hand with this has not yet been fully worked out.

E.R.: *Regarding what you said about the ill-considered comments of certain critics and the lack of serious studies of the technical and theoretical aspects of your music, I am reminded of the complaint of Schubert and Schoenberg, who, to characterise an insistent and badly-informed critic, used the then-unflattering expression, "Rezensent."*

N.P.: What I find most incredible is that it is precisely those critics who used to doggedly defend modern music who are today the most conservative, incapable of accepting any compromise with the past. Isn't that a paradox?

E.R.: *It certainly is, but this paradox is all part of contemporary art. Apart from those who are directly involved, everybody assumes that everything to do with contemporary art is simply an expression of maximum non-conformism. In other words, the supposed qualities of art are attributable to those who talk about it with such apparent competence. With a few exceptions experts on contemporary art are themselves sadly conformist. They are incapable of forming their own opinions and are therefore dependant on the judgements of others, which they passively take on board and formulate with a vehemence and assumed, condescending sagacity in order to cover up for their own lack of genuinely critical thought. When I hear or read how certain people talk or write about music it makes me want to keep silent for ever, but perhaps this scepticism is exaggerated. What I mean is that the sort of behaviour one meets in the cul-*

tural world should be subjected to an in-depth critical analysis. I have always dreamt of something like a treatise on the general psychopathology of writers on culture, these high-profile personages in whose sparse but well-aimed blows we recognise the features of Adorno, Proust, Max Weber, and McLuhan. But now, dear Arvo, I would like to come back to your music and would be glad if we could focus our attention on the Stabat Mater. *In this text, so very old and sparse, you have discovered many nuances of articulation that allow us to read and hear it in quite a new way.*

A.P.: It was the time of the founding of the Alban Berg Trio in Vienna, and on this occasion commissions were given to several composers—among them Alfred Schnittke and myself. My first thought was to use a voice as well, but then I decided to juxtapose two trios, an instrumental trio and a vocal trio, in order to achieve greater balance. This way of making connections between voices and instruments is incidentally a particular characteristic of my way of writing. As I have always done in such cases, I began to approach the text and tried to grasp all its possible aspects. Suddenly I felt that for me the relationship between the short and long syllables of the text was of crucial importance.

E.R.: *So you recognised that the text potentially contains a trochaic rhythm.*

A.P.: Yes, and it stays like that to the end. At the beginning it seemed very monotonous to me, but in fact it isn't, because there are the commas that break up the rhythmic scheme—assuming, of course, that you read the text in the right way. This opened up a large number of possibilities that fascinated me very much. Then I tried to develop this general scheme and to extract all possible combinations from it. As far as the punctuation is concerned, you can find something similar in *Passio* in the instrumental parts that occasionally pick up on the development of the vocal parts, though in this work the method is a little different.

E.R.: *I can understand this fascination with a latent rhythm in the words, but I would still like to ask you how you came to take the text of the* Stabat Mater?

A.P.: I can't remember. Perhaps I took it merely out of the necessity of creating a vocal line.

E.R.: *I recall that your* Stabat Mater *made a very intense impression on me when I heard it for the first time. What moved me most was the beginning of the work with the three string instruments playing in a very high register—the sung text comes later on. This beginning with just the strings was like a cry, and I thought of the* Crucifixion *by Masaccio with the Madonna at the foot of the cross. A red cloth is draped over her shoulders, standing out sharply against the golden background. Her desperate, raised arms are a cry, a cry that rises up towards heaven, just like the entry of the three strings that express a terrible and at the same time unmoving tension, like a cry that would go on for ever.*

A.P.: That is like the prophecy of Saint Simeon to Mary when she brought the little Jesus to the temple, predicting that one day a spear would transfix her soul. In the cathedral of Trento there is also a sculpture of the Mother of God whose breast is transfixed with a sword. In reference to what you've just said, it reminds me of what it is like when two fundamentally different elements meet one another, like lava that has been ejected from a volcano and flows into water. It seems impossible that two so very different elements should meet, but that is just what happens in this work. The text contains immeasurable pain and deep comfort at the same time.

E.R.: *That is exactly what I meant. In this opening, what we hear is a very effective metamorphosis of pain into song. The stringed instruments are pure pain, but immediately afterwards this pain changes to song—thanks to a lightening of melodic tension. There is something mystic in this transformation of a feeling into something else, something that makes me think of a gradual over-layering of two different harmonic spectra, revealing unexpected vistas of sound.*

But now I would like to come back to the rhythmic structure of the work, which stems from the words themselves. The text of the Stabat mater is very homogeneous, conceived after the pattern of pairs of tercets[15] in the pattern AAB - CCB / DDE - FFE with a trochaic rhythm in the background that falls

---

15   It. *terza rima*, an Italian verse form.

away at the end of every third verse. Some verses have three or four words or more. An interesting case is Quis est homo qui non fleret, *an exceptionally long verse. I suspect that the different lengths of the verses provided good material for the musical construction.*

A.P.: Doubtless the text offers starting points for many possible interpretations. Words are not exactly my area, but I will say that I pay increasing attention to the potential content of the text. These mystic words of the Gospel according to John, "In the beginning was the Word," lie at the heart of it all, since without the Word nothing would exist. I believe that this concept should not only be conveyed in the text, but in every note of the music as well, in every thought, in every stone. The roots of our skill lie in this thought: "In the beginning was the Word." We may interpret it in many different ways, but this thought has more to do with the ancient formula that once again takes up the *Summa summarum,* something that is at the same time extremely complicated and incredibly simple.

E.R.:. *After such a profound exegesis I am reluctant to return to a merely technical question concerning the treatment of text in your music. Forgive me for being pedantic, but I have noticed that when setting a text you divide each word, as far as is possible, into individual syllables. This is most important because, since* Missa syllabica, *you use the number of syllables in each word to determine the melodic configuration of the word itself.[16] As we have seen, the metric structure of the* Stabat Mater *is very even, consisting of tercets, each verse normally comprising seven or eight syllables in a constant trochaic rhythm. Thus the number of words that make up each verse and the punctuation are variables that you make use of to achieve musical variety.*

In the literature of vocal music one often finds words that are not set syllabically. In your music that seldom happens, perhaps because you feel the need to give each word its corresponding musical clarity.

---

16   The process applied to the *Missa syllabica* consists in the allocation of a note to each syllable, fixing the pitch of the note on a pre-determined scale. For instance the word *Kyrie* is set to notes of the scale of D and is divided into three syllables set to the notes F-E-D.

A.P.: Exactly, and my *Miserere* is constructed entirely in this way. The work is so structured that for each word there is a catching of breath, a rest, as if someone speaks a word then immediately afterwards tries to gather strength for the next.

E.R.: *Before we talk about* Miserere, *it would mean a lot to me to tell you that I personally regard this work, among all your compositions, as your master-piece.*

A.P.: You don't know how happy that makes me.

E.R.: *Now I would ask you to tell me everything about this work that occurs to you.*

A.P.: I am really not so sure that I can say anything of interest about it, but I can tell you that *Miserere* would not have come about without the help of the Hilliard Ensemble.

E.R.: *You've already told us that this ensemble, with its perfection of intonation and purity of phrasing, represents an ideal model for the performance of your compositions, but how were other interpreters and other audiences able to experience your music? How was your relationship, for example, with the Japanese public?*

A.P.: My first meeting with the Japanese public was in Tokyo Cathedral at a performance of the *Passio*. The work was performed by a semi-professional choir that—interestingly enough—called itself the *Heinrich Schütz Choir.*

E.R.: *A Heinrich Schütz Choir in Tokyo doesn't surprise me, I would even say that is typically Japanese!*

A.P.: The director of the choir had studied in Germany, I think in Berlin, and was a very educated woman, a devoted advocate of German music, and in order to nurture her admiration she had founded this choir. My music was most warmly received and I was told repeatedly that it was Japanese music, although I didn't really understand what they meant by that. They performed the *Passio* in their own way, with a manner of phrasing that was very different from what we are used to, and with an accentuation that comes from their way of speaking. I was astounded, because their manner of interpretation really fit my way of writing. Just imagine, there was even a dog in the choir!

E.R.: *You're joking.*

A.P.: No, really. One of the members of the choir was blind, the man could only move about when accompanied by his dog. During the rehearsals the animal sat right next to him and during some passages it made noises, like cats sometimes do, as if it wanted to add its bit.

E.R.: *That reminds me of a piece by Mauricio Kagel in which a dog is supposed to take part!*

N.P.: The programme booklet for the concert was so detailed that not only was the complete sung text printed, but the entire musical structure of the *Passio* was reproduced as well, in the graphic form of a multiple cross.

E.R.: *I believe that a real point of contact between the Japanese musical tradition and your music is to be found in the role that silence plays in both. The silence of the rest within the Japanese aesthetic tradition does not simply imply the absence of sound. On the contrary. The silence between two sounds is of the utmost importance. It is the moment in which one sound dies to make room for the next—what happens in this silent moment is the most wonderful of transformations.*

A.P.: This reminds me of something I said earlier that approaches the thinking of John Cage. I can't remember the exact words, but I said it more or less like this: "How can one fill the stillness, the silence that follows, with notes that are worthy of this silence—this stillness that has just passed?" There is no doubt about it. Rests are rich in sound.

E.R.: *Precisely this thought illustrates the most profound points of contact be-*

tween East and West. On the basis of the observations that we have made concerning silence, the number of syllables, and punctuation, it would be unthinkable to translate your settings into another language. Your Miserere *in English would be unimaginable!*

N.P.: Certainly, in this case it would be a different work. Arvo once wrote a piece in English, *The Beatitudes,* and the conductor wanted to perform it in Latin. Arvo's only possibility was to write a new piece.

A.P.: That is how *Beatitudines* came about. Of course it is a similar piece, since the structural rules are the same, but none the less there are many significant differences.

E.R.: *Thanks to this fascinating discussion about the meaning of silence we can now turn to the* Miserere. *Right at the beginning of this colossal piece there are many long pauses between the words. These rests are only interrupted by a layer of sound emerging slowly from clarinet and bass clarinet that conjures up an atmosphere of silence and loneliness. These first notes and first words of the* Miserere *evoke a state of deepest loneliness of the soul. I would be grateful if you yourself would comment on the beginning of the work.*

A.P.: Think of a criminal, awaiting his final judgement before a court of law, who is given the opportunity to express his thoughts for the last time. There is not much time for final explanations and he must choose his words with great consideration, since his fate depends on them. Psalm 51—on repentance—plays a central role in the tradition of the Church, as it does within context of any religious ceremony. Each word represents a small weight, an attempt to bring the scales back into balance. Even disregarding the context, every word has its particular value, which influences the rests that follow them. It is a chain, in which breathing in and breathing out are interwoven, hope and despair: that was my original intention. Of course the musical dramaturgy must be determined by the composer, but everything else originates from the text, even if everyone does read this text in a different way.

E.R.: *What then were the reasons for the choice of instrumentation: oboe, clari-*

net, bass clarinet, bassoon, trumpet, and two electric guitars (one a bass guitar), two percussionists, organ, and in addition of course solo voices and choir. A truly unusual instrumentation!

A.P.: This instrumentation originated in a work from the year 1976, shortly before, or at the same time as the birth of the tintinnabuli style. I am glad that here, too, my reflections lead us back to Alfred Schnittke. At that time his *Requiem* was being performed in Tallinn, and I used the opportunity to align the score of *Calix* that I was just writing with Schnittke's *Requiem* so that the work could be performed at the same concert. I recall that my work should have borne the text and the title of the *Dies irae*. However, since it was impossible in the Soviet Union to give a composition a title like that, I had to invent another name and I called the work *Calix*.

This piece no longer exists today, but perhaps it is interesting to know that the basic material—that is to say the scale and the three notes of the triad—like a premonition of the tintinnabuli style, did not as yet follow the style's strict rules, but were asynchronous, which led to many acoustic problems.

I reworked *Calix* according to the tintinnabuli rules and inserted it into the *Miserere* at the words *Et peccatum meum contra me est*. That is the moment of the Day of Judgement. When this section draws to its conclusion—the whole *Dies irae* lasts for quite a long time, about five minutes—I return to the *Miserere* psalm with the words *Tibi soli peccavi, Et malum coram te feci*. As you can see, it is a dramatic digression. To return for a moment to the text of the *Requiem*, I would like to point out another difference, in this case to Mozart, who lets his *Rex tremendae majestatis* vibrate with the sound of terror, while I create a more mild atmosphere, an atmosphere that Mozart only arrives at with the *Salva me fons pietatis*.

E.R.: *There is a written testimonial from March 1999 that touches upon this point and describes the relationship that unites you with Alfred Schnittke. It is a valuable document and I reproduce it here:[17]*

---

17 Arvo Pärt, "Im höchsten Maße feinfühlig: Alfred Schnittke in Tallinn," *Musiktexte: Zeitschrift für Neue Musik* 78 (1999): 41..

I am bound to Alfred Schnittke by a lasting friendship, although we have not often had the opportunity to see each other. In February, 1976, Alfred came to Tallinn for a recording of his *Requiem*, and our meeting in those February days came to be of great significance to me.

In the year 1976 I was in the middle of a long period of searching: for new orientation, for my own language. Already years of retreat and experimentation lay behind me. Now was a time in which my search seemed to be on the brink of bearing fruit.

It was a moment of inner tension between the overwhelming feeling of complete readiness and expectation of the birth of something new, and at the same time a feeling of despair and helplessness in the face of the question of how this new music was to take concrete shape. I was like an up-beat hanging in the air that any moment must descend. Alfred was the first person from outside to whom I opened myself. It was not easy to entrust him with something that for myself had, as yet, neither form nor substance nor name, nor anyone to whom it might be addressed. I could only share all this with someone very close to me, someone with the utmost degree of sensitivity. This person was Alfred.

Alfred reacted very wisely. He made no attempt to judge the material I showed him, but he sensed the situation exactly, understood this phase of my search and determined its course. At the time he gave me just one piece of advice, namely, to put this stage of experimentation to the test of living sound. He advised me at once to realise my numerous sketches in performance and not to stay staring at my sketch books behind closed doors. His words were the help and the midwife I needed—it was as if scales had fallen from my eyes.

Soon afterwards I presented my compositional system, tintinnabuli, to the public. A little later I dedicated one of my first works of these years to Alfred Schnittke. *Calix* (*Dies irae*) in a new version, found its way into my large work *Miserere*. In the year 1977, one year later, Alfred played the part of prepared piano in a concert in Tallinn in which his *Concerto grosso* and the première of my *Tabula rasa* were presented together.

Arvo Pärt

E.R.: *When I heard* Miserere *I was particularly struck by the wonderfully mild atmosphere that resonates towards the end of the work. Of course I could not know that above it all there hovered the shadow of Mozart. However I did notice that, instead of an atmosphere of terror, a warm atmosphere of reconciliation, produced by the sound of the bells, permeates the music. With their harmonic waves these instruments conjure up a sense of distance in space and time that loses itself in eternity.*

N.P.: The text of *Miserere* is a penitential psalm that represents a central hub of the Christian tradition. The author of the psalms—King David—a spiritual giant, a prophet, had sent a man to certain death in war simply so that he could gain possession of his wife, whom he lusted after.

In his despair he wrote this psalm in which he confesses all his wretchedness and weakness. Here we are forced to ask the question: if the greatest prophet of the Judeo-Christian tradition was capable of such crimes, what is a man capable of, any one of us? What dark depths does mankind carry within himself? The 51st psalm has become a symbol of human imperfection. It shows us clearly that one only approaches enlightenment through a sober renunciation of all self-deception and illusion.

I remember that Tolstoy and Goethe both expressed similar thoughts in their diaries. There is no crime that they would not have been capable of committing. It impressed me deeply that two personalities of this sort, and of such different character, harboured similar thoughts.

Now back to Arvo's music: I believe that with his choice of such subjects he is asking himself so-called "eternal questions": What is man?

A.P.: Precisely at the moment when man recognises and admits his own insignificance, then comes the moment of his inner liberation: the "resurrection."

N.P.: This air of reconciliation you spoke of with which the work ends is the ultimate key to the meaning of the *Miserere*.

E.R.: *One more question about* Miserere. *In the first part, to the words Am-plius lava me, you interweave several voices, inserting interpolations from the instruments between each word and the next. Here, more explicitly than in other places in the score, you employ the hocket-technique[18]—typical of the Ars Nova. There are many other moments in which you use a sort of hocket in your music, but here the reference seems clearer than ever.*

A.P.: In a certain sense the tintinnabuli style is itself a form of hocket. All you hear at the beginning is a single voice on the clarinet, but from that moment on the weave becomes closer, other voices join in a *stringendo poco poco*—yes, it is true, it all gives the impression of a hocket.

E.R.: *There is another subject I'd like to go into briefly, since it made a particular impression on me. The third section begins with the words* Quondiam iniquitatem meam ego. *First we hear a bass voice, very low, over which the other men's voices enter in higher registers. At this point one can scarcely tell whether or not this sound really is a human voice. It could also be an instrument, as was often the case in medieval polyphony, where the part of the Tenor was given to an instrument. As the voices enter they move upwards like a spiral, while the atmosphere remains very dark. At the words* Et peccatum meum contra me est semper *the women's voices join in and the canon grows gradually denser until the* stringendo *becomes a* stretta. *It is like a description of hell.*

A.P.: That is just what it is, as the text of the *Dies irae* describes. Thus a picture emerges that shows how this moment is interpreted in the tradition of the church.

E.R.: *You mean* Omnia scriptum remanebit?

A.P.: Yes, the repentance emanates from a single person, always in the first person singular, an "I" as in the "I" form of a literary work. So in *Passio* there are four voices singing the part of the Evangelist. Here in *Miserere* the same thing happens: there are five singers, but everything comes from the same person.

18　Hoquetus: a type of composition in the music of the Ars Nova (ca. 1200—1400), whereby two adjacent voices are broken alternately by rests, interlocking to form a single line.

E.R.: *The manner in which you resolve the* Dies irae *musically—I mean the mensural canon with its descending a-minor scales moving simultaneously in five different tempos, (each tempo doubles the note values so that the slowest is 16 times longer than the shortest)—this mensural canon offers a imitation of chaos, a carefully constructed chaos, as if it were organised by precise machinery.*

A.P.: An infernal machine.

E.R.: *Every unit, every particle of the music is perfectly organised, but the overall impression is that of a highly effective mimicry of chaos. In musical literature there are many such machines with their precision mechanisms, in a line of thinking that reaches from Bach through Shostakovich to Ligeti, and finds its iconographic equivalent in the drawings of M. C. Escher.*

Let me now turn to the four instrumental interludes in the third part, the third in particular, played in a fast dance tempo.

A.P.: There are also interludes of this kind in *Stabat Mater*. These are just— I'm not sure quite how to put it—just music: music we need, like light, like air.

E.R.: *During this period, in 1989, you wrote the* Magnificat.

A.P.: I do not remember exactly how this work came about. Originally there was a commission for a boy's choir in Berlin. You know, with such practical matters and in awkward situations in general I retreat and let my wife deal with it all.

N.P.: It's good hearing you say things like that in front of the microphone!

E.R.: *It is a piece that only lasts for a few minutes. Perhaps Mr. Davico,[19] who had the opportunity of singing in the choir in your* Magnificat, *would like to say something?*

---

19 Nicola Davico, composer, musicologist, and German linguist, was present during these conversations with Arvo Pärt. He undertook the transcription of the recorded conversations.

NICOLA DAVICO: It was the first time I had heard or sung your music. I was very impressed by the beginning of the work: this C that moves towards D-minor. Everything moves in such a light manner and is so closely woven about this C. I didn't know that the piece had been written for a boy's choir.

A.P.: It is usually performed by a mixed choir.

N.D.: What I do remember is this lightness that permeates the piece, the transparency of the writing.

A.P.: Yes, it is very simple: everything moves very slowly about this axis.

N.P.: Although it presents remarkable difficulties in intonation and perform-ance, the *Magnificat* is frequently performed.

A.P.: Tönu Kaljuste said recently that there is no choir that has not sung this work. Perhaps he was exaggerating, but I have noticed that it is one of my most frequently performed pieces.

E.R.: *Along with* Solfeggio *perhaps the most often performed piece.*

A.P.: No, absolutely not, *Solfeggio* is difficult for everyone. There isn't even a good recording of the work on the market.[20]

E.R.: *If I am not mistaken, over the last few days we have touched on your* Mozart-Adagio *for piano trio. Could you tell me how this piece came about and what influence particular interpreters had on the work?*

---

20 *Solfeggio* is a five minute long composition for a cappella choir written in 1963. The four voices (soprano, alto, tenor, bass) limit themselves to singing the seven notes of the scale of C-major ten times in succession. The layering of the various octaves, the delicate dynamic variation and the skilfully handled textures of varying tone colour generate an astounded enthusiasm in the audience at every performance. The composer is quite right in considering the piece to be one of his most difficult to interpret. Any attempt to fathom and explain the secret of this piece would experience similar difficulty: a piece that in its absolute purity seems, more than others, to harbour the mystery of Arvo Pärt's music.

A.P.: In fact this piece originated in the great friendship between myself and Oleg Kagan and Natalia Gutman, with whom I used to work a good deal. Making music with both these wonderful musicians was a beautiful experience. Then Oleg died unexpectedly. It was a very great loss. I considered him to be one of the greatest Mozart interpreters on the violin. So I decided to send him a final greeting with a composition permeated by the sound of his beloved Mozart. I took the Adagio of a Mozart piano sonata[21] and used it for a piece for violin, cello and piano.

E.R.: *Who were the interpreters at the first performance?*

A.P.: The Joseph Kalichstein Trio gave the first performance at the 1992 Helsinki Festival, which commissioned the piece.

N.P.: Arvo's intervention in Mozart's score is at the level of what one might describe as the micro-dimension. However, these minute changes place the work in an unfamiliar perspective, out of which new tensions can arise. Of course on the level of performance the question of style is difficult to resolve. On the one hand one must play Mozart in a somewhat distanced manner—while remaining within a Mozartian style. On the other hand one must be aware of Arvo's alterations in the score and interpret these correctly.

This work is a perfect example of how minute movements can result in consequences on a much larger scale.

This work of Arvo, in combination with Mozart, has for my ears a quiet and tender radiance, as if it was a loving embrace between them both (Arvo, Mozart) and the dedicatee Oleg Kagan.

E.R.: *In this case the concept of a micro-dimension takes on a revealing significance. This a piece by Mozart in which Arvo intervenes at the micro-dimensional level. As he himself points out, not one note of the original is missing in his reworking. Olivier Messiaen, who dedicated a sharp-sighted study to Mozart's piano concertos,[22] confirmed the fundamental significance of the*

---

21 Sonata KV 280. The Adagio in f-minor (in 6/8, siciliana rhythm) is saturated with a deep melancholy.

22 *Les 22 concertos pour piano et orchestre de Mozart* (Paris: Librairie Séguier, 1990).

micro-dimension in these works, particularly in the field of rhythm. According to Messiaen, the fineness of Mozart's rhythmic scansion results from the interplay of modulation and accent—thus also of word accentuation. The fact that these accents are not explicitly notated in the score and must be deduced from melodic context, harmonic progression, and many other factors explains how enormously difficult it is to perform Mozart well. Bad Mozart interpreters—and according to Messiaen, and not only according to him, there are many of these—are bad because they are unable to enter into this micro-dimension. This explains why Arvo, in working with a piece of Mozart, decided to engage at this level. All we have said up till now—and I think here predominantly of the relation between word and music that we have discussed at length—is substantiated here in Messiaen's enlightened vision of Mozart.

But now I would like to return to our discussion of the interpreters, the other musicians who have worked together with you with great sensitivity and enthusiasm. Personally I have always thought that the relationship between composers and their interpreters is one of the most interesting aspects of the creative process in music.

A.P.: For composers it is a great gift to have excellent musicians at their disposal, and in this regard I have been very lucky. I worked for a long time with Gidon Kremer, Neeme Järvi, Tõnu Kaljuste, Saulus Sondeckis, and above all with the Hilliard Ensemble, and I am sure I am forgetting many others here. New music usually confronts both composer and interpreter with many questions and problems, so one must be able to rely on very precise work in its preparation, and this must happen as a collaboration. One cannot simply meet for the rehearsal, perform the concert, and then say goodbye, never to meet again. Both must share a common desire to create something new together. The most important and at the same time most difficult moment is the beginning. The tintinnabuli style often confronts the soloists and members of the choir with problems. They are confronted with unusual leaps, such as are normally found in instrumental music.

I remember that David James, the counter tenor of the Hilliard Ensemble, once said that finding one's way into this music was like learning to ride a bicycle: at a certain point one learns not to fall over, then everything works.

E.R.: *What you allude to here has been a problem for almost all composers of the last 60 years at least. Only relatively recently has the conviction generally taken hold that for good performances one needs specialised ensembles. That doesn't mean that new music must be limited to a few interpreters and a small audience, but it does require a certain intellectual curiosity and a generous portion of enthusiasm—which is only to be found in those musicians who are most strongly attracted by things new. The power of routine, with its many disciples, is also very much a part of musical life. This large passive front must be confronted by a small but dynamic and enterprising group of musicians like those whom you have mentioned as your favourite interpreters.*

It is thanks to them that musical life in the past century has not been bound to an ever decreasing budget, and the figure of the interpreter has enjoyed a new intellectual profundity, in keeping with our own time. A remarkable example of this deeply innovative mentality manifested itself in recent years in the concert series Domaine Musical *that Pierre Boulez founded in Paris to support performances capable of realising the qualities of the music of Anton Webern, which at that time was largely disregarded. Over the years the* London Sinfonietta, *the* Ensemble Intercontemporain *the* Ensemble Modern *and many other very good groups of musicians have sprung up almost all over the world. Thanks to them the contemporary repertoire has proliferated in a manner commensurate with its value.*

A.P.: I personally think groups like these should become models for other ensembles. A CD recording with these courageous musicians can be an enormous help for anyone who wants to get to grips with this music. When I think of my *Tabula rasa*, a piece that to begin with proved to be very problematic, I must admit that these problems have now disappeared. Thanks to the CD recording of Gidon Kremer and Tatjana Gridenko there has been a general frame of reference as to how this piece should be played. And I must admit that when I prepare a new work with musicians who have no experience of my music sometimes I begin to doubt the value of my own work.

N.P.: In some cases Arvo has even wanted to destroy the score! But one must bear in mind the difficulties with which the musicians have to struggle when they play these pieces. The problem is that they must succeed in producing sound in quite a new way. The training that they receive in academies does not always help them here. An interpreter must be aware that if she is unable to play a passage in simple fifths cleanly, the sound will just not be as open as it should be.

E.R.: *We have spoken of the impossibility of translating your works into different languages. In 1994, in* Litany *you used the English language for the first time. What was the experience of using this new language like? Are there connections between the languages that you have used in your work, since words, with their phonetic and rhythmic characteristics, are the most important formative elements in your music?*

A.P.: There are many very obvious external differences between languages. In English for example the majority of words are monosyllabic, while in the Finnish language there are incredibly long words. I love Latin because it is somewhere in between: there are many long words in this language that contain a whole world, like *misericordia* for instance.

E.R.: *You marvel at Latin, as Stravinsky did.*

A.P.: Yes, I feel a sense of admiration, but I believe that Stravinsky had a more distanced, cooler approach. The starting point for *Litany* was a commission from the Oregon Bach Festival. It was natural that I should choose the English language—that is the way things are normally done. The text, very well known, is by John Chrysostom, the great poet, theologian and philosopher of the 4th century. I don't remember whether *Litany* was my first encounter with English, but anyway a number of works based on English texts followed. *Litany* was a completely new experience for me. In using words of so few syllables for the construction of the melodic line I had to find other ways than those I normally employ to extract music from words or sentences.

The structure of the text of *Litany* helped me a lot, because it itself represents a self-contained musical form. The text is built up of twenty four short sentences, short prayers . . .

E.R.: *. . . One for each hour of the day.*

A.P.: One can also see the division of the prayers into twelve for day and twelve for night. In this way each sentence can be seen as a self-contained thought, like links in a chain. This all means that the central point shifts with each thought and that the constructional axis is constantly moving.

E.R.: *At the beginning a violin plays a very high E, a note that acts like a sort of astral body, a metaphysical idea. Can one see it in this way?*

A.P.: Certainly, why not?

E.R.: *A model like that of the* Stabat Mater, *that we spoke of earlier. It has a similar opening, but it is full of dramatic meaning. Here is no trace of pain, perhaps because the prayer opens the doors to an atmosphere of mysticism. That was my first reaction.*

A.P.: I cannot offer you anything objective here: it is possible that there are many interpretations, and if I were to add something, perhaps this would act as a barrier to the spontaneity of a listener's response.

E.R.:. *Perhaps I expressed myself badly. I meant to say that we can only view a work objectively through its structure. I thought I might be able to approach the work with greater objectivity if you were to disclose some basic elements of the piece's construction.*

A.P.: At the beginning a voice sings a beautiful prayer and in the same moment the answer comes from heaven. I limited myself to realising what is already there in the text. Before mankind can ask God for help, God is already there with him. The time in which such things take place is not our time. Perhaps this temporal shift we spoke of earlier happens at a subconscious level, but it is so, even if that sounds paradoxical.

E.R.: *You have represented two states of being, the human and the divine, immeasurable but none the less bound one to the other. Fundamentally the fate of each individual is bound to the question of transcendence. When I mentioned the beginning of* Litany *that impressed me so much, I vaguely sensed a simultaneous presence of elements both near at hand and distant, and now I recognise in this the representation of transcendence—that also contains within it the* condition humano. *The instruments echo the voices and in this manner divide each prayer into the three phrases we discussed.*

A.P.: Something similar happens in *Miserere*, where the instruments alternate with the voices to form an echo.

E.R.: *There is another aspect of the score I would like to go into, namely the question of symbolism. You have said that these 24 prayers represent the hours of the day, and indeed the hours are marked with precise musical symbols: an inheritance of baroque figuralism.*

A.P.: To be honest I don't exactly remember how everything is constructed, but a few times in the second half the timpani enter to remind us of the time of day, at other times it is the bells, like a real clock.

E.R.: *A similar thing occurs when the solo voices start to intone the prayer, with the choir in the background that moves through descending scales. Of this slow cascade at first only one note is sustained, then two, then three and so on, until each section of the text—each prayer—has been counted. The sustained notes in the choir act like a sort of sounding hourglass.*

A.P.: That's quite right. You know sometimes one doesn't notice things and it all happens subconsciously. Now, looking back it seems natural to interpret things in this way, but at the time I didn't think of it like that.

E.R.: *You really didn't think of it? It thought it was intentional.*

A.P.: Often things like this happen intuitively.

E.R.: *In the practise of his art the artist often follows many symmetries intuitively and only through long experience does he learn to handle them skilfully.*

I must admit I have the greatest admiration for the finale of this score. After the amen *begins the* sfumato—*over an increasingly slower and lighter repetition of the motive and a gradual descent into low registers and dark sonorities. At the end the bass voice is scarcely audible: a wonderful finale!*

A.P.: The meaning of this finale is intimately connected to the last prayer, to the final words. The individual at prayer gives himself up into the hands of God without a struggle: "Your will be done." There are no reproaches, only reconciliation.

E.R.: *When I think of the repetition of all these amens that close the work I am reminded of the* Sept Visions de l'Amen *of Messiaen, seven different meanings of the word* Amen. *Do you also feel that so much meaning can be attached to these words?*

A.P.: Certainly, in fact many more than seven.

E.R.: *Let us now turn to the* Berlin Mass, *a composition from the year 1990, that—if I remember correctly—was premièred during a church service in Berlin.*

A.P.: Yes, that's right. The *Berlin Mass* was commissioned by the *Verband der Deutschen Katholikentage* and was performed for the first time in the St. Hedwig Cathedral in context of a service.

E.R.: *That would have been impossible in Italy. I have often tried to persuade the Catholic authorities to allow a musical mass—chosen from the most sober and simple of the repertoire, such as that of Stravinksy—to be included in the liturgy, but I have never succeeded. The one exception that I can think of is a mass by Mozart conducted by Karajan in St Peter's Cathedral, celebrated by the Pope.*

N.P.: It seems to depend on the decision of individual priests. The Bishop of Essen, Dr. Hubert Luthe, for example, wished for a new composition by Arvo that could be included in the mass. One of the more recent examples is the *Salve Regina* that is also dedicated to Bishop Luthe.

A.P.: There is also an organ piece, *Annum per annum*. It was performed on occasion of the jubilee of Speyr Cathedral. I divided the piece into eight parts so that it would be possible to perform them as parts of a purely instrumental mass.

E.R.: *There is another recent work of yours that was the result of a church commission, namely* Kanon Pokajanen *for a cappella choir, composed for the 750 year celebration of Cologne Cathedral. If I am correctly informed, you worked for a very long time on this extensive piece, a few years I believe, during which time you gradually familiarised yourself with the Old Slavic text. This* Kanon Pokajanen *also has a long history behind it. Would you like to tell it to us?*

A.P.: It is a text that is more than a thousand years old, stemming from a very old tradition. When one dedicates oneself to such texts, not as an art form or literary text, but as an existential document, one begins to understand that they are offering us a path to follow. To begin with I did not intend to set the whole text, just some parts, but then I received a commission and I decided otherwise, even if the commission wasn't specifically for the setting of this text, and definitely not for one in Old Slavic.

E.R.: *The text is certainly difficult to read and I believe it is incomprehensible even for Russians.*

A.P.: Yes, that is true. It is the language of the Russian-Orthodox liturgy, but the relationship between this language and Russian is analogous to the relationship between Latin and Italian. Of course the setting of such a challenging text is a great responsibility, not less than the writing of a passion. I decided to attempt it because in my innermost heart I felt the wish to come to terms with this text. In my opinion it is the interpreters who have the most difficult task, who have to sing a cappella with perfect intonation for about ninety minutes.

E.R.: *The text of this canon has a very precise structure. It consists of nine odes, and each ode is divided into various parts. Its construction includes musical directions*

that follow a structure derived from Byzantine texts. According to Egon Wellesz[23]
there are in each ode eight different modes that follow liturgical models. Is there
any of this old musical construction of the odes left in your Kanon Pokajanen?

A.P.: No, for centuries now this canon text has no longer been sung, just
spoken.

N.P.: In the music of the Eastern Church there are eight keys, or modes. Their
characteristic quality lies in the way that each text is coupled to a fixed form
of musical representation. And each unit of text and music is defined as one
of the eight church modes.

The text of the sixth church mode became the basis of the *Kanon Poka-*
janen. In his composition Arvo did not follow the musical representation
that belongs to the text.

E.R.: *Then according to what you say, it is true that in this old tradition, too, the*
text precedes the music to which it is sung. I would now like to read a quote of
yours in which you say: "It was this Canon that showed me clearly how much
the choice of a language predetermines the character of a work—to such an ex-
tent in fact that the whole construction of the composition becomes subjugated
to the text and its laws, if one allows the language to "make its music."[24]

There is an important document by Arvo Pärt himself concerning this essen-
tial relationship. It is included in the notes to the record of Kanon Pokajanen
that the Estonian Philharmonic Choir made for ECM Records under the direc-
tion of Tönu Kaljuste.

Many years ago, on my first encounter with the Russian Orthodox
Church, I came across a text that left a profound impression upon
me, though I was scarcely able to grasp its meaning. It was the *Peni-*
tential Canon. Since then I have returned repeatedly to these verses
as, little by little, they began to reveal their content to me. Two compositions for choir (*Nun eile ich*, 1990, and *Memento*, 1994) were

---

23 Egon Wellesz, *The History of Byzantine Music and Hymnography* (Oxford: Claren-
don Press, 1961).

24 Arvo Pärt, *Kanon Pokajanen*, ECM 1654/55. (1998).

my first attempts at approaching the *Penitential Canon*. Then I decided to set the text in its entirety—from beginning to end. This gave me the chance to remain within its field of influence over a long period—in fact I was not able to escape this influence until I had finished work on the score. I experienced something similar during my work on *Passio*.

I worked for more than two years on *Kanon Pokajanen*, and the time we spent "together" was a very fulfilling one. Perhaps that is the reason why this music is so close to me.

In this composition, as in some other of my vocal works, I attempted to use the language as a starting point. I wanted to give the words the opportunity of choosing their own sounds, of drawing their own musical line. So—to my own surprise—a music arose that was permeated with the strange character of this special language used only in liturgical texts.

It was this *Canon* that showed me clearly how much the choice of a language predetermines the character of a work—to such an extent in fact that the whole construction of the composition is subjugated to the text and its laws, if one allows the language to "make its music." The same compositional structures, the same way of dealing with words leads to different results in different languages. One may compare *Litany* (English) with the *Kanon Pokajanen* (Church Slavic). In both cases I used strictly structured, identical compositional rules, but both works turned out very differently."

Arvo Pärt

A.P.: The language of the Slavic Church also has its particular characteristics, as does English—we spoke about this earlier. For me each language has, so to speak, its own world with its own history, character, intonation, and many other associations. When I choose a text all these aspects influence the compositional process, consciously or unconsciously. I don't know what would happen if I were to decide to use a Chinese text, but I am convinced that in each case it is necessary to recognise the special characteristics of a language with which we want to work. The quote I referred to is right, but there is much more that could be said on the subject.

N.P.: When Arvo begins a new work he is very much influenced not only by the language in which the work is to be sung, but also by other external events connected with the commission.

E.R.: *Fathoming a language in order to extract from it the structure of a musical composition is something that has always fascinated me, and in my opinion has been given insufficient attention. Many of the most fundamental differences in form and style that music assumes in various countries have their origin in the inherent musical qualities of their particular languages. However, in the face of a work like* Kanon Pokajanen, *I have the feeling that that there was something on the part of Arvo that I can only describe as a more profound submersion in the acoustic and spiritual substance of the language. It may be that this higher identification resulted from the opposition between the forceful expression of the* Hirmos[25] *and the quiet note with which the words "Have mercy upon us" are uttered.*

This same juxtaposition of an emphatic manner with which one proclaims one's faith and the humility with which one confesses one's weaknesses, is to be found in other works as well, but is seems to me that in this long, ancient prayer this is taken to an extreme. I can't imagine what the acoustic experience of the performance in such a large space as Cologne Cathedral must have been like.

A.P.: From an acoustic point of view it was not a happy experience.

N.P.: It would be better if no music was performed in this cathedral.

A.P.: Perhaps one can perform music there, but for us it was a problem because the whole sound just went straight upwards. And the most unpleasant thing was the cold: it was the beginning of spring and it was still very cold.

N.P.: I would like to add one small comment. To confront an audience with this text, and that in Old Slavic, is a very audacious undertaking, and may

---

25   Each ode of the Canon begins with the *Hirmos* (Greek ει'ρμόσ, model, chain) that bears an important thought from the nine biblical songs (mainly from the Old Testament) customarily sung during Matins.

seem to be a bit of an imposition today. In ninety minutes we run through every weakness of mankind, and I remember that in America, straight after the performance, a journalist referred to one sin in particular and asked Arvo whether he had committed it. That was of course a very naïve question. This text is not about one person in particular, but about mankind in general. Anyone who dares to look into his own soul and manages to recognise his true self—and that is just what happens in *Kanon Pokajanen*—this person should become eternally generous in dealing with the weaknesses of others.

E.R.: *I agree with you, although pointless questions like the one posed by the American journalist crop up in every age. It amuses me to imagine the strange questions that Haydn might have been asked before the first performance of his* Creation. *I don't doubt the power of a work like* Kanon Pokajanen *to involve its audience. I think that many people are ready for such a spiritual meditation. The need for spirituality is very great in our time. However uncertain and confused this time may be, and in spite of the prevalence of the tendency to give in to the seductiveness of superficiality, it cannot be denied that in the long run fruitful ground appears for every artist. The concert that we heard in the mountains at dawn the other morning is the best demonstration of this. So many people made their way out at daybreak to listen to a music they believed would be capable of fulfilling so many expectations.*

This brings us to the end of our conversations. It only remains for me to thank you for the kindness and patience with which you have answered all my questions.

CASTEL TESINO, JULY 2003

1954 | Photo: Private Collection

1960 | with Heino Eller | Photo: Private Collection

1962 | Photo: Armin Alla

1963 | Eesti Raadio | Photo: TMM Archive

1977 | Tabula Rasa | Photo: Private Collection

1977 | Helle and Andres Mustonen, Arvo and Nora Pärt | Photo: Kalju Suur

1978 | with Alfred Schlee | Photo: Private Collection

1978 | with Oleg Kagan | Photo: Harri Rospu

1980 | Nora and Arvo Pärt at the Carinthischer Sommer Festival | Photo: Private Collection

with Alfred Scnittke | Photo: Nora Pärt

Christmas in Vienna with Immanuel and Michael | Photo: Richard H. Smith

with Manfred Eicher | Photo: Robert Masotti

1992 | with his children Arina, Triinu, Immanuel, and Michael | Photo: Nora Pärt

2000 | Rome | Photo: Vivianne Purdom

2000 | Royal Academy of Music, London

3 つの 悲 歌 (オルガンのため)
TRES LAMENTATIONES
菅野浩和
Hirokazu SUGANO
オルガン・ソロ 武久源造

アルヴォ・ペルト
ARVO PÄRT
ヨハネ 受 難 曲 （日本初演）

JOHANNESPASSION

イエス (バリトン) 宮原 昭吾
ピラト (テノール) 佐々木正利

福音史家/合唱 ハインリヒ・シュッツ合唱団
HEINRICH SCHÜTZ-CHOR, Tokyo

指揮 淡野 弓子
Leitung：Yumiko TANNO

ヴァイオリン 小野 萬里
オーボエ 川村 正明
チェロ 伊藤 耕司
ファゴット 堂阪 清高
オルガン 武久 源造

22. Ev.	Illi autem dixerunt:	彼らは言った。

23. C H O R : Jesum Nazarenum.
合唱／祭司長たち：ナザレのイエスだ。

24. Ev.	<18,08>Respondit Jesus:	イエスは言われた、

25. J E S U S : Dixi vobis, quia Ego sum:
ergo me queritis, sinite hos abire.
イエス：「わたしである」と言ったではないか。
わたしを捜しているのなら、この人々は去らせなさい

26. Ev.	<18,09> Ut impleretur sermo, quem dixit:	それは、（次の様に言われたイエスの言葉が）実現するためであった。
27. Ev.	Quia quos dedisti mihi, non perdidi ex eis quemquam.	「あなたが与えて下さった人をわたしは一人も失いませんでした」
28. Ev.	<18,10>Simon ergo Petrus habens glodium eduxit eum: et percussit Pontificis cervum:	シモン・ペトロは剣を持っていたので、それを抜いて大祭司の手下に打ってかかり
29. Ev.	et abscidit auriculam ejus dexteram. Erat autem nomen servus malchus.	その右の耳を切り落とした。手下の名はマルコスであった。
30. Ev.	<18,11> Dixit ergo Jesus Petro:	イエスはペトロに言われた。

31. J E S U S : Mitte gladium tuum in vaginam. Calicem quem dedit mihi Pater, non vibam illum?
剣をさやに納めなさい。父がお与えになった杯は、飲むべきではないか。

32. Ev.	<18,12> Cohors ergo,	そこで一隊の兵士と
33. Ev.	et tribums, et ministri Judaeorum comprehenderunt Jesum.	千人隊長、およびユダヤ人の下役たちは、イエスを捕らえて

	partiti sunt vestimenta mea sibi:	「かれらはわたしの服を分け合い、
159. Ev.	et in vestem meam miserunt sortem. Et milites quidem haec fecerunt.	わたしの衣服のことでくじを引いた」兵士たちはこのとうりにしたのである。
160. Ev.	<19,25> Stabant autem iucsta crucem Jesu Mater ejus,	イエスの十字架のそばには、その母と、母の姉妹、
161. Ev.	Maria Cleophae, et Maria Magdarene.	クロパ（クレオファ）の妻マリアとマグダラのマリアとが立っていた。
162. Ev.	<19,26>Cum vidisset ergo Jesus matrem, et discipulum stantem, quem diligebat,	イエスは、母とそのそばにいる愛する弟子とを見て、
163. Ev.	dicit matri sue:	母に言われた。

164. J E S U S : Mulier, ecce filius tuus.
イエス：女の方、これがあなたの息子です。

165. Ev.	<19,27> Deinde decit disciplo:	それから弟子に言われた。

166. J E S U S : Ecce mater tua.
イエス：お前のお母さんだ。

167. Ev.	Et ex illa hora accepit eam discipulus in sua.	そのときからこの弟子はイエスの母を自分の家に引き取った。
168. Ev.	<19,28>Postea sciens Jesus quia omnia consummata sunt, ut consummaretur Scriptura, dixit:	この後、イエスは、すべてのことが今や成し遂げられたのを知り言われた。

169. J E S U S : Sitio.
イエス：渇く。

170. Ev.	<19,29> Vas ergo erat positum aceto plenum.	そこには酢い葡萄酒を満たした器が置いてあった。

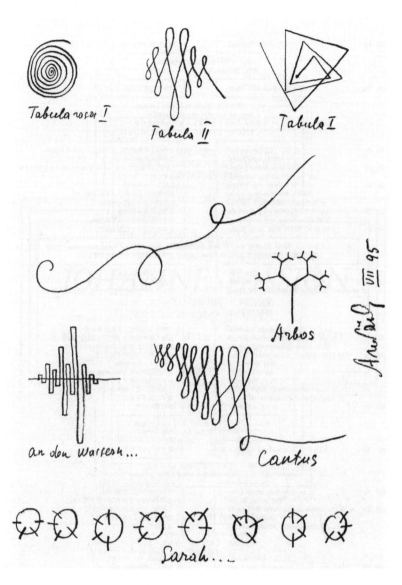

From 1995, Arvo Pärt's graphic representation of his work

2003 | with Leopold Brauneiss | Photo: UE

2003 | Castel Tesino, Arvo and Nora Pärt, Enzo Restagno, and Nicola Davico |
Photo: Roberto Masotti

2003 | Castel Tesino, with Enzo Restagno | Photo: Roberto Masotti

2010 | Istanbul | Photo: Mart Einpalu

2010 | Istanbul | Photo: Ali Borovali

1978 | Illustration by Heinz Valk

Tintinnabuli: An Introduction

Leopold Brauneiss

Leopold Brauneiss, born in Vienna in 1961, studied musicology, history, music pedagogy, and piano at the University of Vienna and the Academy of Music and Performing Arts in Vienna. After a period as a teacher at a grammar school in Vienna he taught at the M. Hauer Conservatory in Wiener Neustadt (piano and, until 2007, music theory). Since 2004 he has taught music theory at the University of Vienna, and since 2006 music theory and instrumentation at the Felix Mendelssohn Bartholdy University of Music and Theatre in Leipzig. His compositions lie mainly within the field of chamber music. He has published widely, particularly on the subject of Arvo Pärt's tintinnabuli style.

Introduction

After the première of his *Credo* in 1968, as scandalous as it was success-ful, Arvo Pärt came to the realisation that the compositional techniques of his avant-garde works—dodecaphony and serial organisation in connection with areas of improvisatory freedom, *collage* technique, and sound mass composition—had led him into a cul-de-sac.

Years of searching followed: for a sound-world valid beyond the fashiona-bleness of that *en vogue,* for a music whose strength lies in renunciation, in a form of concentration achieved through a reduction to basic essentials. It was a search in which the study of old music, from Gregorian chant to the vocal polyphony of the 16th century, played an important part. Finally, in 1976, he composed a series of works in a new style that the composer him-self called *tintinnabuli* (Latin, small bells). Characteristic of this style are:

- limitation to the simplest basic elements of tonality: triad and scale;
- a new type of compositional texture based on the allocation of these basic elements to different voices: melodic voices (M-voices), based on scale segments, and so-called tintinnabuli voices (T-voices) con-sisting exclusively of notes of a triad, the so called tintinnabuli triad;[26]
- A new musical *ductus*, mainly in slow tempos, whereby each note is given individual weight and significance.
- A "highly formalised compositional system"[27] in which the melodic and harmonic progressions are the result of a network of interre-lated rules, which can partly be expressed as formulae.

---

26 Compare: Chap. II, *Addition of voices.*
27 Arvo Pärt. *Zu Summa*, in *Nähe und Distanz. Nachgedachte Musik der Gegenwart,* ed. Wolfgang Gratzer (Hofheim 1996): 13.

An analysis of the formulae of this music, with their simple single-figure mathematics, might at first sight appear unproductive since these formulae can only explain the mechanics of the music, not its effect. "The schematic element of the composition, combinations of numbers . . . all that acts as a semi-translucent, protective wall: one penetrates quite easily, but the piece does not give up its secrets."[28] And yet, taken to its logical conclusion, such a conviction would inevitably silence any discussion of his music all together—or at best lead one to approach the tintinnabuli style in evocative, poetic language—a form of music criticism that has, in its turn, become the subject of scientific study.

However, a study of the history of the music's reception without reference to the compositions themselves and the intentions of the author that are manifested within them would be incomplete. Although the impact of a work of art may ultimately never be ascribed to precisely definable causes, we must not abandon the attempt to connect cause and effect as far as this is possible, deriving meaning from compositional processes, treating rational understanding as a prerequisite for an understanding of that which transcends the boundaries of rational thinking. In an attempt to connect the rational with the irrational, it is this author's conviction that we must, above all, confront a concept that is realised wordlessly in the tintinnabuli style itself: the principle of a reconciliation of opposites, which—viewed from a central point—converge to form an overriding unity.

28   Wolfgang Sandner, *Der stille Ton. Zu den Orchesterwerken Arvo Pärts*, in *Studien zur Instrumentalmusik*, Lothar HOffmann-Erbrecht zum 60. Geburtstag (Frankfurter Beiträge zur Musikwissenschaft 20), ed. Ange Bingmann, Klaus Hortschansky, Wilfried-Kirsch (Tutzing 1988): 513.

I
1 (One)

"The complex and many-faceted only confuses me, and I must search for unity. But what is it, this one thing, and how do I find my way to it? Traces of this perfect thing appear in many guises, and everything that is unimportant falls away."[29]

Arvo Pärt

The One

The search for "the one"—for unity—and for possible ways of reaching this goal, is doubtless a central concern of the tintinnabuli style. In a more general sense the idea of a search for simple principles governing the treatment of musical material ties in seamlessly with the philosophical idea of a search for the single source from which all surface variety ultimately springs. Within the tintinnabuli style this idea is connected with the moral and aesthetic motive of the search for perfection and—unifying all of these—the theological idea of the search for the divine.[30]

Arvo Pärt has described this path to an all-embracing unity through a variety of illuminating images. In an interview from the year 1968 he compared it to the mathematical process of reduction. "It is more or less as if we tried to reduce a number (for example 1) in the form of an extremely complicated fraction with many intermediary calculations. The way to a solution is a tedious and strenuous process: however the whole truth lies in the reduction. If we assume that a similar solution (the number one) connects all the various fractions (epochs, human fates), then this one is more than the solution to a single

---

29 Wolfgang Sander, booklet to CD *Tabula rasa*, ECM New Series ECM 1275 CD 817764-2 (Munich 1984).

30 Descriptions of the religious character of the tintinnabuli style must inevitably remain superficial unless they address the area in which all threads become interconnected—including those of the music itself.

fraction. It is the correct solution to all fractions (epochs, human fates), and it has always been. That means the greater and clearer the recognition of this final solution (the number one), the more 'contemporary' the work of art."[31]

In a more recent interview, Pärt has spoken of a "nucleus" that must be reached: a picture that invites associations both with the nucleus of the biological cell—with its chromosomes containing the sum total of all information—and with the nucleus of the atom—with its potential inner energy that is released when it is split. "In the compositional process I always have to find the nucleus first from which the work will eventually emerge. First of all I will have to get to this nucleus."[32]

The Single Note

"One": in music, this is the basic unit of melody and form in its most simple, "singular" manifestation. The simplest element of music—yet, like cell and atomic nucleus, in itself divisible—is the single note.

Pärt's much-quoted sentence, "I have discovered that it is enough when a single note is played beautifully,"[33] indicates the renewed significance attached to each individual note within a simplified, transparent structure. One might say that each note, down to the slightest eighth note, is of equal importance to the composer—something that has far-reaching consequences for performance practise. However, it would be wrong to assume that an interpreter should attempt to awaken these few notes to musical life through individual expression. A performer's goal—difficult enough as it is—is to present these single notes and harmonies as they are—through "beautiful performance"—and as such allow them to unfold their effect. And in turn the listener, too, must become attuned to the smallest differences between each note and the next.

Arvo Pärt has admittedly not written any one-note pieces, since this "mo-

31 Saale Kareda, "Dem Urknall entgegen": Einblick in den Tintinnabuli-Stil von Arvo Pärt, in Kirchenmusikalisches Jahrbuch 84 (2000): p. 61.
32 Geoff Smith, Sources of invention: An interview with Arvo Pärt, in The Musical Times (Autumn 1999): 20.
33 Sander, booklet.

notony" in the melodic movement would have to be made good through a still more sophisticated structuring of the parameters of timbre and rhythm. This would go against Pärt's aim of simplifying all structural means to an equal extent. The experience of the single note in isolation, perfectly resting within itself, can however be integrated into a composition consisting of many notes. Apart from the traditional compositional technique of pedal point, the single note appears in its most overt form at the beginning or end of a work. Three examples illustrate this phenomenon.

At the beginning of the first movement (*ludus* = game) of the double concerto *Tabula rasa*, the silence is broken by the note A (A and A) played fortissimo by both solo instruments. Not only do these notes establish the tonic, in their extreme registers both notes also mark the boundaries of the musical "playing field" to be filled with movement by the subsequent melodic curves as they grow successively further and further outwards from the note A. The process is concluded when the unison returns, immediately before the final chord, as the last note of two arpeggios converging in contrary motion through the entire tonal space (Ex. 1).

Ex. 1

The single note not only opens musical space, it also sets musical time in motion. Contrary to the amorphous silence before the beginning of the work, the silence of the long rest that follows the first note is a measured stillness: it returns repeatedly, successively shortened, throughout the course of the movement while the melodic movement extends continually outwards, both in time and tonal space. (Section 1, melodic movement one note + 7/2 rest, section 2, melodic movement includes additional notes above and below the central note, in total 3 notes, + 6/2 rest. Compare: *Addition of formal elements: Tabula rasa.*) Space becomes time.

The piece finishes as it began: with a single note followed by silence. However, the musical significance of this closing silence is now very different. One by one the instruments have left the field—its boundaries are determined by the ranges of the instruments. The solo double bass is left alone and is the last to play the note E, supertonic to the tonic D. In the continuation of the D-minor scalic movement and in an imagined continuance of the omnipresent D-minor triad, the listener envisages this note—or this chord—carried over into the silence of the bars' rest that close the piece. A precisely composed, resonant silence of a different kind is the goal of the composition *Silentium*. The sound transcends the boundaries of the physically audible so that—to risk a rather blatant concept—one might speak of metaphysics in sound.

Como cierva sedienta also begins with a single note, D-flat in the low register of the soprano (Ex. 2). It grows out of the silence in *pianissimo* and fans out, changing colour with the addition of various instruments (bar 2, viola and bells, bar 3, alto flute and cello, two octaves below the first note of the inversion of the soprano melody), then is harmonically intensified by an added A-flat, a fourth below and fifth above, finally becoming part of the diminished seventh chord E–(G)–B-flat–D-flat (2nd quarter note of bar 3, cello/harp). Here, too, is a music that unfolds from a single note. However, in every way it acts in a manner diametrically opposed to the beginning of *Tabula rasa*. There the abrupt change between *fortissimo* and silence, here the continual flux of minute transitions. There the homogeneous string sound, here a mosaic of single elements of different timbre.

The harmonic situation is different, too. As in *Tabula rasa*, subsequent events confirm the opening single note A as tonic. The harmonic situation in *Como cierva sedienta* is labile, shifting between the F-minor triad and the diminished seventh chord. Only little by little does the note F crystallise out as a tonic: a music searching for a unified sound and a unifying tonic, mirroring the words of the psalmist who compares the yearning for God with the thirst of a deer ("As the deer yearns for fresh water, so does my soul for you, O God").

Ex. 2

In *La Sindone*—the title refers to the Turin Shroud—the single note is not the starting point as it was in the previous examples, but rather the goal of the musical events. In the closing section the music rises in a sort of musical ascension to the highest registers of the strings. As the border is crossed, each instrumental group successively falls back into the note E. As the tonic of the piece and root note of the E-minor tintinnabuli triad, this E has been present in the background throughout the work; now it finally moves forcefully into the foreground in all its weight and significance as the real origin of the music. Although this closing, triumphal confirmation of the tonic corresponds to the traditional idea of a tonal close, such an ending is seldom to be found in the works of the tintinnabuli style. More often, these works do not consciously close at all, but rather are left open-ended, or lose themselves in silence. Similarly, in *La Sindone*, a quiet postscript follows the resounding *tutti* unison. The work closes with a quiet triad on E, with minor and major third sounding simultaneously: we do not yet see simple truths clearly, the mystery of the Turin Shroud remains, as do the mysteries of death and the resurrection.

The Single Chord

The setting of the poem by the German Romantic poet Clemens von Bretano, *Es sang vor langen Jahren*, for alto (counter tenor), violin, and viola, opens not with a single note, but with a single A-minor triad (bars 1-6). Like the note A in *Tabula rasa*, the chord is separated from subsequent events by rests (bars 7–8, excluding upbeat), and closes the work, again separated from the six verses of the poem by silence (bars 219–224). Like a musical version of the stereotypical fairy tale opening line, "Once upon a time," it frames Brentano's picture that Pärt translates into music: a spinster mourning for her lost companion. The chord acts as a barrier dividing memory from the present, leading us into the distant past—to a German Romantic narrative, whose lyrical "I" in turn also looks back "many a long year." In the correspondence of beginning and end, the chord is part of an overall symmetry that transforms the temporal progression of the composition into a static picture in the memory.

First Half, Bars 1–113 (113 Bars)

Bar 1–8	Bar 9–113
8 bars, A-minor triad and rest	105 bars, verses 1–3 and instrumental passage

Second Half, Bars 114–226 (113 Bars)

Bar 113–118	Bar 219–226
105 bars, verses 4–6 and instrumental passage	8 Bars, rest and A-minor triad

The Single Note, Repeated

If the isolated single melodic note represents the single event—the "one" in its most radical form—repetition of the single note may be seen as a way of clinging fast to this "one," fixing it to a single pitch. We find syllabic singing on one note in two of Pärt's works: a setting of the 121st (120th) psalm, and *My Heart's in the Highlands*, after words by Robert Burns. In both works melodic stasis is supplemented by continual instrumental movement that repeatedly transports the single note into different musical contexts, allowing it to appear in perpetually shifting guises. The backbone of this movement in *Wallfahrtslied* (*Pilgrims' Song*) is a descending chromatic scale. In *My Heart's in the Highlands*, the F-minor scales in the bass extend in a wave-like motion (F–G–F–E-flat–F–G–A-flat–G–F, etc.), similar to the wave motion that lies behind both movements of *Tabula rasa* (Ex. 15).

In both pieces the note of recitation alternates between the different notes of a tonic chord: verses 1–4 of the *Wallfahtslied* are sung on the root note of an E-minor triad, in verses 5–8 the fifth (B) follows (the dark, low B to the words, "the moon by night"), whereas the final words of verse 8, "from now until eternity," find their way back to the tonic. The notes of recitation in *My Heart's in the Highlands* rise up during the first verses through the F-minor triad (Verse 1 f', verse 2 a-flat', verse 3 c") to return in the final verse to their point of departure, (two lines a-flat', two lines f'). This technique of juxtaposing melodic progressions—in this case instrumental progressions—with a repeated note as "vanishing point" of a tonal phrase offers another way of integrating the aesthetic experience of the single note as isolated phenomenon—the "one"—into the overall musical picture.

Recitation of a single note is reminiscent of certain types of sacred music, such as liturgical recitation in Gregorian chant. Such associations seem to be confirmed by the significance Pärt himself attaches to his discovery of Gregorian chorale during the time spent developing the tintinnabuli style. "Gregorian chant was for me the first impulse [on the path to the new beginning represented by the tintinnabuli style]. It was unadulterated admiration. I had never heard this music before. And when I came across it by chance, I knew: this is what we now need, what I now need."[34] However, this does not mean Gregorian chant acted as a direct stylistic or compositional influence. It acted more as a catalyst in his search for a music of reduction, concentrated in its sparseness, a catalyst that helped to establish the character of a tintinnabuli style that already existed in Pärt's imagination but as yet lacked concrete shape. It provided the impulse that allowed him to dare the step to monody as the starting point of his composition. The compositional means that Pärt discovered and developed to recreate the effect which Gregorian chorale is capable of producing on the listener of today are among the other aspects of the tintinnabuli style to be discussed in Chapter 2.

---

34 Roman Brotbeck, Roland Wächter, "Lernen, die Stille zu hören. Ein Gespräch mit dem estnischen Komponisten Arvo Pärt," *Neue Zeitschrift für Musik* 3 (1990): 14 ff..

The One and the Many

Though analysis may demonstrate the role of the single musical unit—the *"one"*—in all its manifestations in Pärt's works, the question of the motive behind his search for simplicity and fundamental unity still remains to be answered. The following quote leaves no doubt that Arvo Pärt saw his music as an opposite pole to the state of the world today, in all its ever-increasing, multi-layered complexity. "These are now my musical thoughts, my tone colour, my loud speakers, my volume, my vocabulary, my breath. The world has a wave as well, but it never coincides with where I am. There must be a counter-balance between the waves. If things are moving in one direction, we must move in the other."[35]

If we see the task of art as being to constantly hold up a mirror to the present condition of the world, then we must inevitably regard Pärt's tintinnabuli style, and its vision of music as a counter-balance to the multiplicity of this world, as being out of touch with the spirit of the time. The only fitting musical analogy would be a style of "radical plurality," such as the German philosopher Wolfgang Welsch sees as fundamental to the postmodern world. Within the context of Welsch's thought the concept of *unity* appears as mere wishful thinking and is seen as something to be overcome: "Radical postmodern plurality breaks with these unifying brackets that hope for a totality that can only be achieved in totalitarianism."[36]

We might argue that the idea that art must aesthetically *duplicate* the world is itself one sided, in that it precludes the possibility of a concept of art as a *balancing counterpart to*—an opposite of—the real world. As the comparison with the mathematical process of reduction quoted earlier suggests, the reductionism of the tintinnabuli style does not result from the "raising up of something to a seeming absolute that is, in fact, merely particular."[37] It is the declared objective of the composer to focus the existing variety of the world into a single point, or conversely, to gain a variety of musical progressions from a musical structural core within a framework which varies from work to work.

---

35   Heinz Josef Herbort, "Wohlklang und Stille. Der in Westberlin lebende estnische Komponist Arvo Pärt", *Die Zeit* 1.2.(1985).
36   Wolfgang Welsch, *Unsere postmoderne Moderne*, 3rd ed. (Weinheim, 1991): 4/6.
37   Ibid., 5.

In his typology of artistic plurality, Wolfgang Welsch has himself spoken of a monadic type, for whom the "creation of complexity from simplicity"[38] is characteristic. His characterisation of postmodern architecture might well describe the web of voices in Pärt's compositions, as we shall show in detail later, whether one chooses to call them postmodern or not: "Repetition, reduplication and inversion create in their interplay a structure full of provocation."[39] It is not about a "one" referring to nothing but itself, but rather the relationship of this "one" to the many: a fundamental compositional and aesthetic problem that has been solved in a special way in the tintinnabuli style.

II

$$1 + 1 = 2$$
$$1 + 1 = 1$$

The One and the Second

Following the hermeneutic principle that things may be understood only when one recognises the problem to which they offer a solution, all the compositional details described below can be seen as circling around the question of how a second phenomenon may be added to a first (1+1=2), this "second" being as closely related to it as possible, so that ideally it appears not as something different, but rather as another aspect of the first (1+1=1). A music of small steps, minute differentiations, in which a second phenomenon exhibits as simple a relationship to the first as possible. This basic principle of *stepwise addition* determines both the shaping of the single melodic parts—the horizontal dimension of the music—as well as the layering of several voices—the vertical dimension.

---

38 Ibid., 129.
39 Ibid., 128. The concept of provocation (Ger. Irritation) refers to the innovative character of the unusual treatment of familiar tonal material.

The Scale, the Melodic Modes

The simplest form of melodic motion is the step to a neighbour note.[40] When this motion is repeated, it produces the scale—the intervallic principle that lies behind the melodic progressions of most of Pärt's works. Preferred are the various types of minor scale to which an additional augmented second may be added. Occasionally we find a chromatic scale (*Wallfahrtslied*) or a whole tone scale (*Passacaglia* for violin and piano Ex. 23).

Like a straight line in geometry, a scale is infinite in both directions. By fixing either a first or final note it is given a one-sided border. A systematic description of all possible scalic movement away from or towards such fixed notes (to be called *central notes*) results in four melodic types: a scale may descend or ascend away from a central note or, descending or ascending, move towards it. Paul Hillier has described and numbered these possibilities as modes.[41] As these four melodic modes are in principle of equal importance, to place them in a numerical order is inevitably arbitrary. Instead, I have suggested making the melodic curve visible through the use of arrows, defining the central note as a particular degree of the scale employed. In Ex. 3 we assume the note E' to be the fifth degree of A-minor, (A-minor 5). If there is an arrow in front of the number (↗5, ↘5), the central note stands at the end of the scale segment, with an arrow following the number (5↗, 5↘) we assume the note stands at the beginning.

Ex. 3

Stepwise Addition

If scales have a boundary at one end—a central note—other mechanisms are required to determine how far the scale moves away from this note. The principle of stepwise addition come into play in the early tintinnabuli pieces.

---

40 The biblical "neighbour" to whom is due a respect equal to that afforded to oneself.
41 Paul Hillier, *Arvo Pärt*, Oxford Studies of Composers (Oxford, 1997): 95.

Scale segments continually extend, in that each time the segment is repeated, another note is added.

The simplest scenario is illustrated by the beginning of *An den Wassern zu Babylon saßen wir und weinten* (Ex. 4). The descending natural or äeolian A-minor scale extends stepwise outwards to the range of a fifth. One could say that the final notes of each scale segment (or the extended notes that precede them) form a scale in their own right—in other words, two scales interlock. This can be schematically described as follows, whereby the numbers after the double dots refer to the stepwise extension of the scale outwards from the central note to the lower fifth:

A-minor 5↘:1–2→1–5

Ex. 4

The melodic progression becomes more elaborate when the process of addition is based on the combination of several modes, as at Figure 4 of the same work: A-minor ↗1 and ↘1 and at Figure 5 in the opposite order: A-minor ↘1 and ↗1, resulting in an inversion of the melodic line from Figure 4 (Ex. 5). In the following formulae, the square brackets indicate that the additive extension refers to the bracketed combination. Since in these scale segments the central note (1) is at the end, in the formulae referring to the extension of the scales the 1 has been added after the larger numerical value (4–1 and not 1–4 as before).

A-minor [↗1 + ↘1]: 1→ 4–1 and A-minor [↘1 + ↗1]: 1→ 4–1

Ex. 5

In the wave-like ascending line upon which both movements of *Tabula rasa* are based, all four melodic modes are interconnected. The extension in the second movement loses itself in the endlessness of silence:

D-minor [1 ↗ + ↘1 + 1↘ + ↗1]: 1–2 → ¥

Ex. 6

The additive principle is clearly recognisable in the following sixteenth-note passage from *Adam's Lament*, though here it is more complex in that it combines different patterns within a confined tonal space. After an extension according to the pattern G-minor [1↗+ ↘1]: 1–2 →1–5, an accelerated diminution follows. It is difficult to pin-point in a formula, since it lacks a central note: 5 notes upwards, 4 downwards, 3 upwards, and finally, filling the bar again, three notes descending instead of a further reduction to 2 (Ex. 7). The entire last bar is then repeated and the three-bar model transposed up a third eight times. C is altered to C-sharp (in the transposed sections F becomes F-sharp), when the line ascends further, reminiscent of the practise of *musica ficta* in "old music."

Ex. 7

The Role of the Text

While such additive extensions play an important role in his early tintinnabuli pieces, Pärt soon found within the texts he was setting a further regulative principle that could be used to govern the distance a scale-segment moves away from its central note. This simple principle is particularly important in the works of the mid-nineties. With a strictly syllabic setting, the number of syllables within each word dictates the number of notes of the scale employed. Once the central note and the melodic modes have been fixed, the music "writes itself," as Pärt repeatedly put it in conversation. At the beginning of the *Gloria* of the *Missa syllabica*, for example, D-minor ⟋5 in the alto and D-minor 1⟍ in the tenor are paired, the monosyllabic words (in the example, "in") are sung on the central notes D' (D-minor 1) and A' (D-minor 5), words of two syllables ("De-o") result in two note segments of the scale to A' or away from D', words of three syllables ("Glo-ri-a, ex-cel-sis") result in three note segments and so on (Ex. 8).

Ex. 8

This short extract illustrates the pronounced significance of the text in this work. By "translating" the formal structure of the text into music, the text—a constantly varying succession of words and sentences of different length—becomes the focal point of the composition: the knot that ties together all the various musical strands.[42] It is the unifying element—the "one" —that, rather than exclude diversity, creates variety from unity. Varying groups of words of different length result in ever changing combinations of scalic segments within the melodic line, even when texts are made up of a number of verses.

---

42 The way in which the music follows the formal characteristics of the text rather than describing its content is reminiscent of avant-garde techniques that make use of text as sound material, independently of its semantic meaning. The deconstruction of language associated with these techniques is transformed into its opposite in the works of Pärt: in its respect for the body of language in all its subtleties it automatically embraces the comprehensibility of the text while at the same time transcending it.

In this way the objective formal parameters of the text shape the music. In addition to the number of syllables, other textual features determine the disposition of the melody, most significantly the accentuation of the words and the articulation of the text, as described by the punctuation. In this way music and language are as tightly interwoven as they supposedly were in ancient Greece and, if in a different way, in Gregorian chant. The main difference is admittedly that the music requires mediating rules to overcome the division between these two, formerly unified elements. Differentiated rules are applied to specific characteristics of the linguistic original, such as the speech melody, whereby the rule requires that the highest note is given to stressed syllables within the word. In the following extract from the *Kanon pokajanen* (Ode III) the melodic line consistently rises to the stressed syllable, falling afterwards in stepwise motion to the same final note E', upon which the monosyllabic words are recited. According to the position of the stressed syllable within the word, these notes lie at different pitches and are of different length: if the last syllable is accented it falls to the final note E-sharp and is extended to 2 quarter notes. If the second to last syllable is stressed it is set a second above the final note E' and is extended to three quarters in length (in the example, "u-ter-di-viy"). If the third to last syllable is stressed the note is a third higher and 4 quarters long (in the example, "ka-mye-ni") and so on. The last note before a comma is also four quarters in length (in the example, "Tvo-ye-go," Ex. 9).

Ex. 9

As we shall show, the interplay of rules conceived individually for each work goes far beyond principles derived from the language itself. The elaboration of this network of regulatory principles that determine the character of each individual piece and its relation to text thus defines the creative area into which the composer as *subject* has retreated.

When Arvo Pärt speaks in interviews of the objective character of his music, rooted in its strict adherence to self-imposed rules,[43] one should not misinterpret this as referring to a form of aesthetic existentialism that leaves notes and sounds to a life of their own and relinquishes the composer's responsibility to give them shape. However, the concept of objectivity does point towards an attitude whereby the *ego* is allowed to retreat, not in order to destroy it, but to open it to outside influences—in this case to that of language.[44] The belief that a restraining of the ego, enabling it to accept outside forces, will lead to self-perfection, is ultimately a religious attitude. The religious character of the tintinnabuli style is thus founded in the basic principles of its construction and is not limited to surface details such as the use of sacred texts, slow tempos, or the like.

This fact is no doubt of greater significance than the question as to whether specifically Orthodox characteristics can be seen in the music. Such characteristics have supposedly been recognised in the music's reliance on the power of recitation of religious texts or its renunciation of a foreground exegesis of textual content, a "praying in notes" such as is characteristic of J. S. Bach. It is doubtless tempting to deduce a direct influence from the fact that Pärt, baptised as a Lutheran, converted to the Orthodox Church at the time of the development of the tintinnabuli style. However, we may only responsibly claim that some specific details, such as the word-music relationship described above, correspond to the spirit of Orthodoxy. It does not follow from this that Pärt's encounter with the religious philosophy of the Orthodox Church was the cause for the stylistic turn to the tintinnabuli style.

---

43 "Before I choose a rule I have a clear idea of what I want to express. I feel the need to retreat and to present something objective." Klaus Georg Koch and Michael Mönninger, "Klangwelten der Langsamkeit und Stille," *Berliner Zeitung* (1st/2nd March 1997.) "But I entrust the text not only with the rhythm of the music, but also the intonation. Each step is determined by the text. It is not the result of so-called inspiration, it is almost something ‚objective." Helga de la Motte-Haber, "Klang und Linie als Einheit," *Controlling creative processes in music - Schriften zur Musikpsychologie und Musikästhetik* 12, ed. Reinhard Kopiez, Wolfgang Auhagen (Frankfurt am Main, 1998): 232.

44 Pärt's aphorism about the problems of composition—an aphorism that can easily be misinterpreted in isolation—is better understood in this context: "When there is nothing you want to say, know your place . . . you are nobody . . . and write." "Arvo Pärt Tintinnabuli—Flucht in die freiwillige Armut", *Sowjetische Musik im Lichte der Perestrojka*, ed. Hermann Danuser, Hannelore Gerlach and Jürgen Köchel (Laaber 1990): 270.

The Addition of Voices

We return to the basic principle of addition. In the combination of several voices the question of minimal differentiation is allied to the question of unity of harmonic structure: how to combine with a voice a second voice, intimately related to the first, yet, in the most simple and unified way possible, resulting in an independent harmonic quality capable of producing unique interrelationships? The conventional means of parallel movement and inversion come closest to the ideal of greatest possible interrelatedness. We see them both combined in the following example from *Triodion* (Ex. 10).

Ex.10

However, quite a different technique of building up a polyphonic structure from a single line was to prove stylistically defining. Indeed it came to lend its name to this style. According to their position in relation to the melodic line (according to Hillier: M-voice = melodic voice) notes of a specific triad are allocated to the individual notes of this M-voice. The nearest note of a chosen triad may be added either above or below a melody note (in "first position," according to Hillier +1 or -1 Ex. 11a), the *next but one* note of the triad may be added either above or below ("second position" +2 or -2, Ex. 11b) or notes of the triad may be added by alternating between the nearest note above and the nearest note below (+1/-1 Ex. 11c). These possibilities may be used variously in combination (Ex. 11d +1/-1 and -1/+1).

Ex. 11

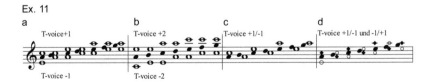

In this way the texture is made up of melodic voices and voices constructed exclusively from notes of a triad. For the latter, Pärt's term *tintinnabuli voices* has become standard terminology. Such triads, sounding throughout a composition, are reminiscent of the ringing of church bells: "After about five minutes [the approximate length of *Cantus*] the sound of church bells no longer results in the impression of individual strokes, but rather that of a chord. This is what I mean by the medieval term 'tintinnabuli,' meaning *ringing*, or *bell music*, which I simply took from the music dictionary." Consequently the triad that is "rung" in these voices is referred to as a tintinnabuli triad— or generally, since in some more recent works the triad is replaced by the diminished seventh chord, simply as the tintinnabuli chord.

Schematically one may describe the T-voice that is allocated to a M-voice as T (superscript) with a designation of its position: A-minor M^{T+1} would be a melodic voice with a tintinnabuli voice in first position above, whereby the "A-minor" defines both the notes of the melody—the key of A-minor—as well as the tintinnabuli chord—triad of A-minor (Ex. 12a). However, if the tintinnabuli triad is not the tonic triad, it must be separately noted. Ex. 12b shows the same M-voice with an E-major tintinnabuli triad (A-minor $M^{\text{E-Major T }+1}$).

Ex. 12

Though it is a simple enough matter to identify and superficially describe a T-voice, it is difficult to interpret its true role. The texture cannot be pigeon-holed into the usual categories of homophonic and polyphonic. Although an M-voice is added note against note ("punctus contra punctum") it is not a contrapuntal voice in the traditional sense of a voice of equal importance and type moving within a framework of fixed rules as to permissible intervallic relationships, etc., complementing and contrasting with the first voice in its linear progression.

In a fugue of J. S. Bach for instance, the voices have the same amount of notes and rhythmic formulae at their disposal. From these the voices are shaped, differing from one another while at the same time complementing each other rhythmically and harmonically. However a T-voice, in its limitation to the notes of the tintinnabuli triad, is of a principally different quality than an M-voice, and also absolutely dependant upon this voice. In spite of this dependency it is not totally subjugated by the melody—in the way that a single voice of typical homophonic harmony is in thrall of the overall progression. It embodies the harmonic quality of the individual notes of the M-voice. One might define it as the other side of its melodic quality—it is the harmonic dimension of this voice, externalised into a separate part.

The complexity of chords and variety of harmonic progressions that has grown continually over the past 200 years is here reduced to its fundamental unit, the tintinnabuli chord. The formula quoted above, 1+1=1, was coined to describe the curious relationship of M-voice to T-voice, characterised by the way in which opposites are combined to form a greater unity: "It is not harmony in the traditional sense and it is perhaps not true polyphony. It is something quite different. It is as if one might say 1+1=1."[45]

The paradox that a single voice—a horizontal linear progression—comprises a basic chord definable as the sum of notes within a vertical collection, allows the combination of a T-voice and its corresponding M-voice to produce a rich variety of detail. The tintinnabuli chord is not just a kind of drone sounding from beginning to end of a piece. Its omnipresence is felt rather in the constantly shifting groupings of its individual notes. In this way chords of different tension, from pure triads to diatonic clusters, alternate, and all are subject to the gravitational pull of the tintinnabuli chord.

The question of the predominance of a particular voice cannot be answered unequivocally: though the compositional process begins with the formation of a melodic basic line—"Ur-linie"—an M-voice upon which all other voices including the T-voice are dependant, the tintinnabuli voice appears as the overriding element. It might be compared to the colour of a painting against which the drawn lines of the M-voice are set in relief without ever losing their intimate connection to this background.

In the joining of the opposites of T-voice and M-voice, colour and line, sound and melody, lies the potential for tension within tintinnabuli compo-

---

45   Klang und Linie als Einheit, 233

sitions. These opposites are not only interwoven, each is transformed into the other: the tintinnabuli chord appears as line, and in turn the simultaneities result from the addition of individual melodic voices. The result is not emptiness but a serenity filled with inner strength.

One might define these opposites with various antitheses, such as *dynamic (M-voice) / static (T-voice)*, or *subjective (M-voice) / objective (T-voice)*. They embody contradicting characteristics, connected in the tintinnabuli style to form a paradoxical unity. The M-voice, with its linear movement away from and towards the tonic, is dynamic in that it evokes tonal tension and relaxation, particularly evident in stepwise motion. The T-voice, with the notes of the tintinnabuli triad, juxtaposes these dynamic progressions against an unchanging, static level of tension.

To talk of the subjective nature of the M-voice, as opposed to the objectivity of the T-voice may sound surprising, in view of our earlier discussions of the melody's "objective" derivation from the syllabic structure of the words it sets. This description is however only unequivocally applicable to the early instrumental pieces in the tintinnabuli style, such as *Für Alina*, or *Pari intervallo*, whose M-voices are freely invented. Nonetheless, the description of the M-voice as *subjective* characterises an important aspect of the style. In that it consists of more notes than the T-voice and, according to the rules governing its structure, tends to oscillate to and fro about a central note, an M-voice may seem to lack orientation. On the other hand, a T-voice can be seen as possessing an objective quality, since it accompanies the M-voice with the few unchanging notes of the triad, anchoring the M-voice in a tonal framework, appearing to "correct" its excursive melodic caprices. Part and parcel of this duality are the various levels of importance attached to individual notes in respect of their relationship to a tonic and to the notes of the triad.

If the M-voice refers to a structured melodic line formed from the "object" of a text, the subjective element in its invention is doubly limited by objective tendencies: firstly through the objective criteria which lead to its construction and secondly through the allocation of a T-voice.

In examining the relationship between M-voice and T-voice we are again confronted by the phenomenon of the translation of religious content into basic structural constellations within the musical fabric. This is borne up by an aphorism by Pärt, who draws an analogy between the relatively free invention of the M-voice with the theological concept of sin: "My melodies are sins, the tintinnabuli chords the forgiveness of my sins."[46]

In passing, it is worth noting that in two works Pärt has also added a T-voice to quotes from Bach and Mozart. In the final part of *Wenn Bach Bienen gezüchtet hätte*, the beginning of the B-minor Prelude from *The Well-tempered Clavier I* is quoted in *Mozart-adagio*, the second movement of the F-Major Piano Sonata, K 280.[47] In both cases traditional functional harmony and its progressions of varying tension are juxtaposed with the omnipresence of the unchanging tintinnabuli triad. Single added notes are enough to set the familiar tonal harmonies in a new light. This music requires a keen ear able to perceive subtle variations—a listening skill which is of overriding importance for the tintinnabuli style in general.

From the great variety of ways in which M-voice and T-voice may be combined, I would like to highlight just two. The single notes of a T-voice allocated to an M-voice need not necessarily sound simultaneously in a separate part, but may also be introduced within a single voice, alternating with the M-voice to form a single, composite line.

The earliest example of such an interlocking of melodic notes and notes of the tintinnabuli triad is to be found in the *Variationen zur Gesundung von Arinuschka*. In place of a "theme" the piece is based on an ascending and descending A-minor scale (a'–a''),whereby two tintinnabuli notes in first position are placed in front of each degree of the scale, the upper note first as the scale ascends, the lower note first as it descends. The rhythmic differentiation of melodic notes (half notes) and tintinnabuli notes (quarters) results in the rhythmic pattern *short-short-long*. The repetition of this pattern is reminiscent of the rhythmic characterisation of motives in traditional thematic construction. The "answering" of the ascending scale pattern with a corresponding descent of equal length that returns to its point of departure is analogous to periodic phrase-building. In this way

46   Arvo Pärt, *Tintinnabuli – Flucht in die freiwillige Armut*, 269.
47   Mozart-Adagio. Compare Leopold Brauneiss, ". . . *ein lebendiges Zeichen in der Asche suchen"*: *Mozart-Umschreibungen bei Henze und Pärt*, in Wolfgang Gratzer (ed.), *Herausforderung Mozart. Komponieren im Schatten kanonischer Musik*, Schriften zur musikalischen Rezeptions- und Interpretationsgeschichte 2, (Freiburg 2008): 45–58.

characteristics of traditional tonal themes are preserved within a structure created with the strictly formalised means of the tintinnabuli style (Ex. 13).

Ex. 13

On rare occasions a T-voice may even appear without its corresponding M-voice. This may seem surprising, since the progression of a T-voice is utterly dependant on an M-voice. Bearing in mind however that T-voices are principally dominant, M-voices can be seen as simply regulating the areas in which at any given moment the tonal colouration of the T-voice may appear, and—to take the pictorial analogy a little further—the drawn line of melody may be omitted all together, leaving just the background.

At Figure 37 of the *Passio* (Ex. 14) the musical texture is reduced to a single T-voice sung by the solo soprano. The M-voice that makes up the soprano line can be simply deduced from the following rules: with each comma of the text the modi—implying a movement away from or towards the central note—alternate. Within the segments that lie between two commas the melodic direction changes with every word of more than one syllable. Thus *Quia* A-minor 1↘, *expedit*, 1↗ and after the comma, reflected musically in a rest half the length of the preceding word (*expedit*: 4 quarters, rest 2 quarters). *unum* ↘1, *hominem* ↗ 1, *mori* ↘1, *populo* ↗ 1.[48] The T-voice alternates within the section between first position above and first position below (T+1/-1), not however after the comma.

---

48   On the stressed syllable of the word immediately before a comma the quarter note value is doubled to a half note; syllables of a word before a full stop are lengthened to whole notes. A rest follows, then an instrumental diminution of the pattern in the inversion.

Ex. 14

The appearance of a single T-voice in this example demonstrates how the basic principle of stepwise addition may act on another level, namely that of overall formal structure. The addition or subtraction of individual voices may be seen as the most minute formal differentiation between two adjacent sections. The prerequisite for this process is the random combinational compatibility of the voices within the tintinnabuli texture, whereby no one voice plays a predominant role. The bass voice does not support a harmonic progression as in traditional functional harmony, and the melodic substance is not concentrated in the uppermost voice. Though the qualities of M-voice and T-voice may be very different, and the addition or subtraction of a voice may alter not just density but also character of the musical texture, the individual voices are not fixed to a particular position. If the distribution of M-voices and T-voices is strictly regulated, as in *Passio*, any single voice, even an outer voice, may be omitted if so required by the mechanism of the additive process.

Addition of Voices: *De profundis*

In *De profundis* for four-part men's choir, percussion ad lib, and organ, the number of voices employed in each verse increases in a regular manner: the first two verses of the psalm are sung by one voice, verses 3 and 4 by two voices, verses 5 and 6 by three, and verses 7 and 8 by the entire choir. All verses are divided into two parts. The voice(s) of the first half are followed by those voices that lie symmetrically opposite in the score. For example, in verse 1 the highest voice (Tenor 1) sings after the lowest (Bass 2), or in verse 3 after the lowest two voices (Bass 1 and 2) the highest two voices (Tenor 1 and 2). Since verses 7 and 8 are sung by the whole choir, only the order of M-voice and T-voice can be reversed (first half T-voice in the tenors and M-voice in the basses, second half M-voice in the tenors and T-voice in the basses). In accordance with the opening words of the psalm (*De profundis clamavi*) it is the lowest single voice that begins. Out of the opening lament of an individual voice, through the addition of more and more voices, grows a collective lament in a suggestively effective increase of tension which is the result of the relentless logic with which the voices are combined.

	1 part				2 parts				3 parts				4 parts			
verse	1/1	1/2	2/1	2/2	3/1	3/2	4/1	4/2	5/1	5/2	6/1	6/2	7/1	7/2	8/1	8/2
Tn I		M				M		M		M	M	M	T	M	T	M
Tn II				M		T	T		M	T	T		T	M	T	M
B I			M		T			T	T	M		T	M	T	M	T
B II	M				M		M		M		M	M	M	T	M	T
dynamics	p				mp				mf				f		mf	mp
M = M-voice																
T = T-voice																
Tn = tenor																
B = bass																

Addition of Formal Elements: *Tabula rasa*

A discussion of the principle of addition would be incomplete without an analysis of its application in a piece of purely instrumental music, a work that is not based on a text. The melodic formulae of the double concerto *Tabula rasa* that combines all four melodic modi into a wave-like, continually expanding scalic motion, have been previously discussed (Ex. 15a and b). In the first movement (*Ludus* = game), they lead the listener downwards into the limits of audible sound, crossing this border into a resonant silence.

The tonal relationships are simple: the "earth-bound" games of the competing instrumental groups in the first movement (solo instruments and prepared piano) in a dominant A-minor harmony (tintinnabuli A-minor triad) appear to resolve into the tonic-like D-minor of the second movement (D-minor tintinnabuli triad). The transition from one tonal region to another is by no means free of friction, and—as we shall discuss later—creates a zone of harmonic conflict (end of first movement, Figure 9, *Meno mosso*).[49] Apart from this section and the cadenza above the descending A-minor scale immediately preceding it (Figure 7, *a tempo*), every note is derived from the basic melodic formula by combining all the principles of addition so far described. In the first movement the single phrases comprising the peak and trough of the wave are separated and appear in each section of the extension process (figure 1, one note, figure 2, an additional note above and below, etc. The following examples quote section 2). Five different versions emerge: the first four are based on an even quarter-note motion that, with note repetition at beginning and end, fits exactly into one bar (Ex. 15c). These five versions follow similarly in all sections: the string orchestra begins with the canonic fourfold multiplication of the basic form (Ex. 15c), it then appears ornamentally three times in the solo instruments, that is with inserted tintinnabuli notes, firstly in eight notes, then triplets, then in sixteenth notes (Ex. 15d).[50] Interrupting the eight-note pulse, the tintinnabuli note -1 to the root note A is split into two sixteenths (tintinnabuli notes -1 and -3). In the sixteenth note passage of bars 18–19 the eighth note movement is doubled.

Only at the end of each section is the simple melodic line—previously hidden in vertical clusters and virtuoso ornamentation—finally revealed (fifth version Ex. 15e). In the "nakedness" of the single voices of the solo instruments that "only have with them the A-minor tintinnabuli triad of the prepared piano,"[51] the melodic line sets itsself apart from the *concertante* texture which precedes and follows it (4/4, even quarter notes), both in tone colour, through the use of high register, metrically, through the 6/4 time[52], and rhythmically, through the regular alternation of four dotted quarters[53] and four dotted half notes.

---

49 The piece can be seen as basically consisting of a single dominant-tonic cadence transposed into a different dimension. This cadence determines the relationship between the harmonic structure of both movements, though it is not the source of surface detail resulting from the various manifestations of the tintinnabuli triad.
50 The even-numbered segments differ from the odd-numbered segments in various ways.
51 This refers to a quote of Pärt: "So the composer would also like to leave the whole arsenal of modernity behind him and save himself in naked monody, retaining only that which is of the most essential—only the triad." (Pärt, "Tintinnabuli," 269.)
52 Notated is a 6/4 bar. In fact it is in 12/8 time.
53 The even numbered sections begin with dotted quarters and the odd numbered sections begin with dotted half notes, of which the first is shortened to a half note. A T-

Ex. 15f shows the unchanging sequence of these elements within section 2: a two-bar introduction from the strings with half-bar canonic entries, then the virtuoso ornamentation repeated three times in the solo

voice is added only every other four-note group.

instruments. Preceding these is an up-beat scale figure, also extended additively, with its tintinnabuli notes (section 2: note g" with tintinnabuli note e" in first position below, section 3: two notes and so on.) Half a bar after the start of the sixteenth note movement the canon returns in the strings, this time with modi exchanged (A-minor 1↘↗ 1↗↘ 1 instead of 1↗↘1↘↗1) and sequence of entries reversed, followed by the chamber-music-like 6/4 passage with solo violin and piano, and finally the rest, discussed earlier, which is shortened on its appearance in each section.

In spite of the overall dynamic quality of the movement, opposing forces of momentum and inertia are at work against each other within individual sections. After the virtuoso *accelerandi* of the solo instruments, a slowing down of the movement in 6/4 time follows. In the strings the canonic thickening of the texture corresponds to a reduction of the number of instruments as the canon runs itself out. The return of the string canon at the end of the 4/4 section implies a symmetrical disposition that runs contrary to a linear, goal-orientated conception of form. The formal development that begins afresh in each section is similarly wave-shaped, as is the voice-leading of the M-voice.

In section 8 the forward moving process reaches the boundary set by the acoustic properties of music: namely the octave. To cross this border melodically would necessitate the repetition of tone qualities in another octave range. This octave is not, however, the definitive end; it does not mean the final resolution of the various musical conflicts within the movement. After the *cadenza*, in *meno mosso*, another additive process follows in the 1ˢᵗ solo violin that fills this octave with a diminished seventh chord C–E-flat–F-sharp–A (Ex. 16). The second solo violin adds a T-voice to the notes of the diminished seventh chord. The harmonic conflict that arises through the superimposition of these two chords is resolved in bars 222/223, in favour of tintinnabuli triad that proves to be the stronger.

Not the "letter" but the spirit of a traditional tonal cadence—the resolution of tension into a closing chord—is realised here with the means of the tintinnabuli style.

Ex. 16

With the long sustained A-minor triad, the movement finally comes to rest in its tonal point of balance. Only afterwards—at the beginning of the second movement (*Silentium*)—do we recognise that this close is merely a dominant transition to the D-minor of the second movement, which represents the actual resolution of the conflicts of the first movement. Although in this second movement the melodic substance is the same as in the first, everything appears transformed (Ex. 17).

Ex. 17

Through the process of rhythmicizing the basic melodic line—the *Ur-linie*—in the simplest way possible (long:short =1:2) and playing it simultaneously at three different speeds—again, in the simplest possible ratio to one another—the sense of a linear forward movement within the extension process is neutralised. Although each voice progresses continually, movement—multiplied in a sort of proportional canon—is transformed into a sense of spacial hovering, into that motionlessness (*senza moto*), which is demanded in place of a tempo direction. In a reversal of the usual order, the slowest level of the canon with breve (dotted whole note/half note): whole note is given to the 1st solo violin, while the fastest layer, with half-note : quarter is given to the cello. Between them—also in terms of pitch—lies the violin 1 with whole note : half note. The D-minor T-voice joins in, filling the tonal space and the metric units (vla. +2 to Cello, Vln. II -2 to Vln. 1), most predominantly in the second solo violin, with its repeated changes of position (long notes -1/+1, short notes +2/-2.). Arpeggios in the piano mark the place where the 1st solo violin returns to its starting note d''' and gradually become less frequent as the waves expand outwards. In ever expanding circles, the melodic lines pass through a tonal space that finally crosses the border into silence.

Such a weave of individual voices, typical of the tintinnabuli texture, is clearly not easily defined by traditional categories of homophony and polyphony. One might instead describe it as potentiated monophony. What on paper and in the compositional process is an addition of voices has the effect of a potentiation of the *Ur-linie*. Described as a formula, the result is 1^x, whereby the number 1 represents the melodic basic line (*Ur-linie*) and x stands for the additional voices added to it. However many voices are added as the exponent, they do not reduce the significance of the single line, but rather confirm it, in the same sense that 1^x always results in 1. Even the radically simple addition principle, so central to the tintinnabuli style, is ambiguous: the further one proceeds in the description of the simple basic principles of the style, the more multi-layered they appear.

III

$1 = 2$

Unity and Opposites

If in the tintinnabuli style the equation 1+1=2 becomes 1+1=1, then it follows that 1=2. This playful mathematical formulation of an identificaton of opposites, in this case the numbers 1 and 2, may be interpreted as implying that one (1) and the opposing "other" (2) merge into a unity at a higher level. This central idea of a unification of opposites, fundamental to the technique and aesthetics of the tintinnabuli style, might be compared to a chemical reaction in which various elements combine to form a substance with new characteristics.

The metaphor of a chemical reaction offers an illustration of the methods described above in which melody and harmony, interwoven in functional tonal harmony, are first separated into M-voice and T-voice, and then, with the aid of simple rules, combine again to form a new unity. The forces of attraction here at play between fundamentally opposing phenomena, comparable to magnetic fields, express themselves on a general aesthetic level in the provoking ambivalence between old and new, time and timelessness, order and chance.

Old and New

"A strange connection of traditional tonal construction and avant-garde gesture has arisen, a music that seems old, and yet could only have been written today."[54] With these words Wolfgang Sandner described the "strange" aesthetic experience of this music, poised between different eras. Hermann Conen spoke plastically of the way in which Pärt's music frees "the oceanic feeling of timelessness" in the ear of the listener. Then: "His music combines

---

54 Wolfgang Sandner, *Der stille Ton*, 510.

'old' traditional material with the new, as-yet unheard of, in a way that at first confuses, then suspends our sense of time."[55] These experiences are more concretely rooted in the connection of "old" tonal material with the strictly formalised, a-thematic "new'" structural techniques, described in previous chapters.

Tonal material is not treated conventionally, nor does it appear in an alienated form, as in the neoclassical style. Instead, through a novel form of organisation it is brought back to life through a return to its basic building blocks of triad and scale. The old, which was previously *tabu* in contemporary music, appears in a new light, as Armin Brunner describes in a very illuminating way: "A man picks up a discarded piece of glass from the wayside, holds it up to the sunlight, and in so doing is confronted with the whole spectrum of colours in all their luminosity. It could have been Arvo Pärt . . . "[56] A comparison of Pärt's *collage* pieces up to his *Credo* of 1968 shows the variety of ways in which past and present may interact. While for instance in the cello concerto *Pro et contra*, triad, aleatoric textures, tonal harmonic progressions, and twelve-tone rows are brought abruptly into opposition, in the tintinnabuli style old and new are intertwined into an indivisible weave. Here even the terms *old* and *new* become ambiguous. From the point of view of his own personal stylistic development, structural thinking, more concretely the principle of addition, is an "old" characteristic of Pärt's compositional technique that survived the breaks in his style. It is at the core of the serially organised sound textures of *Perpetuum mobile* from 1963 as of the *Cantus in Memory of Benjamin Britten*. This is possible because the relationships or processes which may be expressed in numbers are neutral as far as content is concerned. The process of counting is not dependant upon whether the notes being counted belong to a twelve-tone row or a minor scale.

When in *Credo* fifth is added to fifth to the point of vertical and horizontal dodecaphony, this structural process is not only following the text with all the means at its disposal (*occulum pro occulo, dente pro dente, an eye for an eye, a tooth for a tooth*—a fifth for a fifth), it is also leading the tonality of the quoted Bach prelude into dodecaphony and beyond, into passages of

---

55   Hermann Conen, *Annäherung an den Kern der Musik. Systematische Anmerkungen zur Poetik Arvo Pärts*, in Hermann Conen (ed.), *Arvo Pärt: Die Musik des Tintinnabuli-Stils* (Cologne 2006): 96.
56   Armin Brunner, *Ein Glasstück am Wegesrand* (Zürich).

aleatoric improvisatory freedom within given ranges. Thus, here the additive principle in its simplest form—the addition of fifths—becomes the uniting force that allows the opposites to *diverge*.

Within Pärt's individual stylistic development it is not the compositional technique as such that is new in the tintinnabuli style, neither is it his return to tonality, but rather the exclusivity of his choice of tonal material. This is evident in a comparison of the extrovert drama of the *Credo* and its opposite—the tonal archetypes of triad and scale. Tonality in *Credo* is only conceivable as a quote. Through the proliferation of fifths—the archetypal tonal interval—tonality shifts into atonality, in the same way that the turning screw of unending revenge, "an eye for an eye, a tooth for a tooth," ultimately leads to chaos.

Pärt's experience of "old" music, from Gregorian chant to vocal polyphony of the 16th century, which he first discovered during the years of preparation of the tintinnabuli style from 1968–1976, was doubtless an inducement to risk the step towards a form of tonality that could not only unify opposites but might also embrace the principle of addition. Its influence can be seen in the early tintinnabuli pieces, not only in superficial notational characteristics such as the avoidance of short note values and the absence of dynamic and articulation marking, but also in technical details such as the way that a T-voice with alternating positions (+1/1 or -1/+1) intertwines about an M-voice in much the same way as a *counter tenor* does the *tenor* in a medieval motet. However, with the exception of the third symphony, Pärt never stylistically imitated or quoted this music. Old music was more of a catalyst on the path towards a music whose innovative tonal language is the result not only of a limitation to old material, but also to a subjecting of this material to precise methods of construction.[57]

The short piano piece *Für Alina*—the fair copy is dated 1976—is reckoned to be Pärt's first piece in the tintinnabuli style, and it proved to fit the ethos of the time. To put it in the context of the general cultural[58] development of

57   Compare: Leopold Brauneiss, "Arvo Pärt's Tintinnabuli-Style: Contemporary Music Toward a New Middle Ages?" in *Studies in Medievalism*, vol. 13, Postmodern Medievalism, (Cambridge 2005): 27–34.
58   Hermann Danuser, *Die Musik des 20. Jahrhunderts*, vol. 7 of *Neues Handbuch der Musikwissenschaft*, ed. Carl Dahlhaus, (Laaber 1984): 400.

the period: "Since in Europe the belief in progress on an economic, political, and cultural level was cast into doubt, within the field of art and aesthetics, too, the decades-long rule of the philosophy of Modernism, itself never entirely without enemies, went into a state of crisis. The fundamental premise that art must be new if it is to be considered valid was dissolving, or indeed, reverting to its opposite."

From this point onwards in the field of so-called postmodern architecture, building techniques increasingly involved old formal elements, such as columns. Umberto Eco explained the new significance of historically-inherited elements with the argument "that the past, since it cannot even be destroyed, as its destruction leads to silence, must once more be taken seriously."[59]

However, every artist has his own way of advancing the development of art by casting a look back into the past. The tintinnabuli style, which penetrates to the roots of melodic and harmonic construction, may be seen as uncompromisingly radical in the original sense of the word (radix = root), a concept that is usually—though not neccesarily—associated with the concept of the avant-garde, progressing forward in a linear direction.[60] This radicality of reduction, as well as the music's recognition of the past, explains the opposition of the established art world that it had to overcome.[61]

However, the essential turning point in various areas of the arts that set in during the seventies was most probably due not only to external influences but also to developments within modernism itself. Its characteristic expansion of acoustic material to the limitless possibilities of electronic music, its extension of the concept of musical substance in an increasing use of noise, acoustic events produced as a by-product of "actionism," all these encourage the feeling that everything—or nothing—constitutes musical material; or to

---

59   Umberto Eco, *Nachschrift zum Namen der Rose*, (Munich): 78.

60   If one does not limit the concept of progress to a linear progression with one's back to the past, one may see the tintinnabuli style, provokingly, as not only contemporary, since it recognises the needs of the time, but also progressive in its radical demand for recognition of the past: "If we indeed do believe in progress in music, then Pärt is in his way the most progressive." (Armin Brunner op. cit.)

61   As neatly as the development of the tintinnabuli style may fit into the general historic development of the time, this process was by no means an easy one. What may seem to be a logical development, one which occurred independently in the work of various composers, was for each a step into an uncertain future.

put it another way, that there is no more new material left to be discovered. Material itself therefore becomes inconsequential. Instead, it is the way that this material is given shape by the composer that becomes all important.

As early as the twenties, the Viennese cultural philosopher Egon Friedell said, "There is no such thing as new material; new is always the interplay of spiritual forces."[62] However, if the way of dealing with materials—and not the choice of a particular material which is assumed to demand a specific manner of treatment—is the decisive element here, then the concept of the "New" refers not to the material itself, but rather to the relationship between this material and the way it is shaped. It is therefore not only legitimate to use old material in a new way, it is an overriding necessity if one is to remain innovative. The return to the old becomes a pre-requisite for the creation of that which is new and "contemporary." Friedell's bringing together of the significance of the familiar with the concept of truth, that, as old as it is, cannot and need not be replaced by the new, reads like a description of the tintinnabuli style: "The well-ordered, well-bordered region of truth is small. Only the wilderness of stupidity and mistakes, idiosyncrasies and idiocies, is unmeasurable and bottomless."[63] From here it is only a small step to Pärt's aphorism about eternal truth: "With the existence of the tintinnabuli style I would, in a certain way, like to confirm that the truth of the Lord is eternal, I would like to say that this truth is simple! One would like to take a direct pathway towards it." [64]

Sound and Structure

Sound and structure may be related to one another in a variety of ways. The potential diversity of their interrelationship is further complicated by the fact that the concept of "sound"[65] involves two aspects: sound as *timbre*, determined by the choice of instrumentation, and sound as the simultaneous sounding of more than one note. Both facets of "sound" form a triangular relationship with structure that must be addressed in all its aspects.

---

62   Egon Friedell, *Kulturgeschichte der Neuzeit*, München 101993, 55.
63   Ibid., 55.
64   Pärt, *Tintinnabuli—Flucht in die freiwillige Armut*, 269.
65   In German, Klang means both sound and chord. (R.J.C.)

Within the tintinnabuli style, *timbre* is a secondary phenomenon in relation to structure. Various formulae, choice of melodic modi, and the principle of addition, regulate the pitches independently of tone colour or rhythmic progression.[66] In their abstraction they are unspecific as regards their realisation in sound. This degree of abstraction invites comparison to similar phenomena from very different areas of experience, such as religion and the sciences, or with optical impressions such as the branching of a tree or the contour of a landscape. In this sense for Pärt the true value and mystery of music lie beyond its differentiated realisation in a variety of possible surface textures,[67] and are thus independent of the timbre in which the music appears. "For me, the highest value of music lies outside its colour. Special instrumental timbre is part of the music, yet it's not a primary quality. That would be my capitulation to the secret of music. Music has to exist by itself . . . two, three notes. The secret must be there, independent of any instrument. Music must derive from inside, and I have deliberately tried to write such music that can be played on a variety of instruments."[68] Pitch relationships resulting from mathematical formulae may be represented in sound through a variety of acoustic materials.

This independence between primarily conceived musical structure and its realisation in sound was the reason why many early tintinnabuli pieces were written for a variety of instrumental forces, including the historic instruments of the Estonian ensemble *Hortus musicus*, which premièred the first tintinnabuli pieces.[69]

As in the practise of old music, the border between vocal and instrumental composition is fluid. *Summa,* for instance, may be performed vocally by

---

66   Rhythm is frequently determined by structures that are independent of the melodic progression. The division of the parameters of pitch, duration, and timbre is thus comparable to serial composition. The important difference, however, is that in serial composition all parameters are of equal status, while in the tintinnabuli style pitch is of predominant importance.

67   In an interview with Geoff Smith, Pärt compared this abstract concept of a dimension of depth with geometric structures that become visible under appropriate magnification and that are similar in different substances. (Smith, *Sources of Invention*, 20)

68   Martin Elste, "An Interview with Arvo Pärt," *Fanfare* 11/4 (March/April 1988): 339.

69   At the time in which he was developing the tintinnabuli style, it was these "old instruments" that Pärt had at his disposal. As far as the variability of tone colour is concerned, the original instrumentation of these early pieces cannot be considered "authentic."

choir or solo voices to the text of the *Credo*. It may also be played by a string orchestra, a traditional string quartet or a string quartet with two violas instead of two violins. The various instrumental or vocal forces employed illuminate the structures in different ways. Thus, in an a cappella performance of the *Missa syllabica*, the M-voice and T-voice merge, while in a performance with organ the two sound quite separate, because the M-voice is principally allocated to the choir, and the T-voice to the organ.

The fact that pitch relationships may be realised in various instrumental and vocal guises does not mean that timbre is of no importance whatsoever. Once a particular instrumentation is fixed, timbres within the spectrum of the ensemble are so chosen that the structures may be optimally realised within this instrumental variant. The fact that structure and timbre are conceived separately does not exclude the possibility of a structural use of instrumentation. On the contrary, the additive inclusion of successive voices can be linked to changes in timbre—indeed the additive process would seem to call for just this. In the first part of *In principio* for choir and orchestra we find the block-like structures also differentiated in timbre, and particular instruments play clearly defined roles. Oboes and clarinets double the A-minor triad of the choir while the articulating element of the chord is played as an arpeggio in flutes and high strings and as an unbroken chord by the tutti strings with flutes, bassoons, and horns. The chords that repeatedly interrupt the vocal texture at the commas in the text are played by brass and timpani.[70]

Although instrumental timbre here separates the various building blocks of the structure from one another, it is not an integral part of the essential structural organisation—that is to say, of the interrelationship of triad and scale. Rather does the harmonic organisation of the tintinnabuli style attempt to overcome the opposition between sound and structure that arose in the 20th century. This opposition resulted from the problem that the increasingly structural disposition of music—due to its complexity—had become inaudible: " . . . the structural disposition belongs exclusively to the construction of a composition, it does not itself appear as an audible category. The vision of an identification of sound and structure is absurd."[71]

---

70   At the end of the movement, bassoon and strings intensify the texture.
71   Elmar Budde. "Neue Musik—Neues Hören? Aspekte des Musikverständnisses der Moderne," *Österreichische Musikzeitschrift* 8–9 (2003): 38.

As absurd as this vision may seem in view of compositions of the classical modernist era, it does happen within the tintinnabuli style, though this difficult concept of identity must be differentiated. In an interview Pärt carefully stated that construction and sound are so indivisibly interconnected that; the one factor is always present within the other. "The question is actually what comes first, the sound or the construction. They are both present all the time. You choose a particular construction because you already have a sound, but they are dependent on each other."[72]

This illustrates an important function of the basic principal of simplification: the reduction of the compositional texture to a tintinnabuli chord once more admits a perceptible connection between structure and sound which had hitherto seemed impossible or absurd. As the T-voice consists primarily of a single chord, a static sound emerges that appears to constantly change as the M-voice diverges from it in ever changing ways.[73] Whatever pitch relationships the structural rules regarding M-voice and T-voice may produce, their ever-shifting combination in real sound causes a multitude of different results. Generally speaking, the simplification of both material and structural organisation allows the structure to forge a pattern in sound without further technical mediation that, apart from specific detail, is entirely pre-conceived.

Sound and structure are like two sides of the same coin, strictly bound one to the other.

As opposed to the early serial compositions of the forties and fifties, where timbre—indeed, in Olivier Messiaen's *Modes de valeurs et d'intensités*, also dynamics and articulation—is integrated into the structural organisation, sound and structure within the tintinnabuli style, though inseparably linked like the two sides of a coin, retain their independent identities. However, through the process of reduction, certain sounds and progressions are excluded from the outset. One might say that the composer is searching for structural formulae that are capable of delivering ideal relationships at each moment of the compositional process.[74] To find such an ideal structural formula is not only

---

72   "Microcosm in the Cathedral," *Morgenbladet*, (3rd April 1998) (Swedish).

73   With the M-voice progressing through tonal space and the T-voice insisting on a single, unchanging, "timeless" chord, different temporal structures are interconnected: a further set of opposites that are united in an overriding unity.

74   This formulation refers to one of Pärt's aphorisms, in which he defines prayer as an

impossible, it would make further composition unnecessary, since everything would be ready-made: everything—and nothing—would be possible. So it remains the task of the composer to approach this ideal in different ways in the individual work, creating a specific relationship between individually conceived structural rules and the resultant sound. Finding the optimal relationship is, as the many re-workings of scores show, no easy matter.

Since for the most part sounds can only be altered in accordance with the structural rules that give rise to them, if even after reworking, a composition doesn't "sound right," the only possibility is to discard the work altogether.[75] With the concept of "sounding right," the circle is complete, since in this sense *sound*—in its connotation as a description of notes sounding together—and *sound*—in its connotation as a description of timbre—join. One could say that many tintinnabuli structures have been searching for a long time for ideal conditions in which they might unfold in sound. The choice of a particular instrumentation may necessitate a modification of the structures to adjust them to the timbre at their disposal, as is the case with *Mein Weg hat Gipfel und Wellentäler*, first published as a piece for organ, later as a piece for strings and percussion. In judging what is an ideal sound, theoretical reflection reaches the limit of its usefulness: in music the final instance of judgement can be nothing but the ear itself.

Order and Chance

To alter the perspective somewhat, we may regard this identity of sound and organised structure in the tintinnabuli style as representing a new relationship between order and chance. If, due to its complexity, the structure of a work cannot be perceived, a high degree of order will be understood as chaos. To counteract this problem, one may either build in an element of chance, as is the case in aleatoric compositions, or return to a manner of

---

ideal counterpoint to life: "The ideal polyphony is continuous prayer. This 'ideal' counterpoint is capable of producing ideal relationships everywhere and in everything." (Pärt, *Tintinnabuli—Flucht in die freiwillige Armut*, 269.)

75 Pärt has indeed withdrawn a number of compositions—including large-scale works.

composition that does without overall organisation altogether, and concentrates on individual detail.

Compared with these two possibilities, the third path taken by the tintinnabuli style represents a wilful step forward in the dialectic of order and chance. Shaping a composition from a codex of pre-compositional rules means that it is impossible to realise individual details independently of this codex. In other words, these individual details become in a sense "chance events," in that they are not the result of the composer's deliberation, but merely the "chance result" of the application of rules. When asked whether there are places in his composition that he did not foresee, Pärt answered: "It often happens that combinations appear that surprise me, that I wouldn't have thought of, because this music has quite different building rules. Of course I do choose, and a lot ends up in the wastepaper basket."[76] Again it is the simplification both of materials and rules that allows chance to operate, by setting it clearly defined boundaries. Since the possibilities of sound-combination are limited from the start, fewer potentially unwanted combinations can arise. Thus the tintinnabuli style represents a continuation of that which, according to Helga de la Motte, "is the only aesthetically new principle that the 20th century brought forth," namely "the invention of a principle of permutation that generates unforeseen events."[77]

It is important here to note that chance is not used as a method of generating truly new material, foreseen by no one, not even the composer—as for instance in works of John Cage. Through simplification and the use of familiar tonal material, chance is guided into controlled channels where it cannot turn against the order that brought it forth. Since rules are perceived through the actions of chance, the listener grasps that the individual details, *chance events* though they may be, result from the same fateful threads of the fundamental principles that bind the individual notes together. Once more a conviction that one might call religious is encoded within the musical structure: that which may seem chance is, in a deeper sense, "fate."

---

76 *Klang und Linie als Einheit*, 235.
77 Ibid., 236.

IV

The Development of the Tintinnabuli Style

Over the years the technical resources of the tintinnabuli style have developed in various directions while its aesthetic and compositional principles have remained basically unchanged. However, this development does not imply a linear progression from simple to complex. Each work creates its own particular profile, its own characteristic synthesis of the methods the composer has evolved in dealing with scales and their connection to tintinnabuli triads: a synthesis that strictly avoids a repetition of previous solutions. Within the context of this introduction I would like to highlight just a few aspects of this development.

Differentiation of the Structural Relationship Between Word and Sound

Contrary to the early monolithic tintinnabuli pieces like *Passio* or *Tabula rasa*, the longer works for large forces such as *Como cierva*, as well as the shorter vocal works like *Nunc dimittis,* are constructed from a number of segments, different from each other both in structure and character. The narrative choral pieces which appear for the first time with *Tribute to Caesar* and *The Woman with the Alabaster Box* are freer and employ a more uninhibited use of word-painting. A variety of different rules as to the setting of text is applied: those that fit the melodic progression to the sequence of words and those that impose an independently invented melodic pattern upon the text.

In the following example, from the "piccola cantata" *Doppo la vittoria* (Ex. 18), the melodic lines of bass and tenor are derived from the text according to different rules. The bass only moves from its note of recitation on stressed syllables—descending a second on words of two syllables ("quan-do"), and a third on words of three syllables ("da-van-ti, con-ses-so"), a fourth on words of four syllables, and so on.

Ex. 18

In the tenor, however, the accentuated notes lie at the corresponding in-terval above the central note at the ends of words: with words of more than two syllables, the note B-flat; at the two syllable word "quan-do," the note C.[78] "Da-van-ti" and "con-ses-so" each have three syllables, so the accentu-ated second syllable is given to D-flat, a third above the central note B-flat. Contrary to the bass part, the notes that are omitted through the intervallic leaps are distributed onto other syllables. With the word of three syllables in Ex. 17, this is the note C, which sounds on the first syllable. This results in a three note scale-segment in which the first two notes are reversed (C–D-flat–B-flat).

In addition, all three- to five-syllable words in the bass (as well as the immediately-preceding single-syllable words—in Ex. 18, the word "al") are sung alternately in one voice ("da-van-ti") and two voices—with a lower par-allel fourth ("con-ses-so"). The M-voice in the alto lies a fourth above the half-notes of the tenor[79] at all words of more than one syllable, so that with the quarter movement at double speed the accentuated syllables fall together in alto and tenor. The only T-voice (+1 to the alto) lies in the soprano.

Each individual note is derived from the simple basic materials of triad and scale, but the overall picture is more complex in that the scales do not appear as such, but are re-shaped in a variety of ways. This can be seen in the following soprano *unisono* setting of the first sentence of the prayer of the Pharisees from *Zwei Beter* for high voices a cappella (Ex. 19).

---

78   Words of two syllables are treated in this passage in a different way to words with more syllables.

79   Contrary to the tenor, in the alto single-syllable words are combined with following words of more than one syllable to form a melodic arch—both words being treated as one.

Ex. 19

The M-voice does not follow the text but interlocks two scales in parallel sixths with the corresponding tintinnabuli notes in first position above. The resulting four-note constellations made up of notes of the melody and two tintinnabuli notes sound in an ascending and descending arch form, separating the notes of the scale still further.

This type of melodic structure is reserved for the prayer of the Pharisees, and is thus clearly set apart from the narrating words of Jesus, which are musically structured in quite a different manner: a change of scene that follows the course of the narrative, if not describing the text's specific content. The broad sweeping melodic curve, not content to remain within a small segment of tonal space, strictly follows its own rules, with the result that it can only partly follow the "spirit" of the text—for instance in its rhythmic shape—so that, like the Pharisees, caught in their complacency, it is caught in the letter of the law and misses its "spirit."

A final example shows the broad spectrum of possible ways in which scales may be combined, and how the manner of combination may be determined by the text. At each word of the second verse of *Cantiques des degrès*, a setting of the 120th psalm for choir and orchestra, an F-sharp minor scale ascends towards the accented syllable then falls. In words with an accent in the middle (*a-u-xi-li-um*) this results in an arch-like melodic curve (Ex. 20). This combination of ascending and descending scales is, along with the rearrangement of individual notes of the scale already discussed, a further way of allocating highest notes to accented syllables in imitation of speech melody.

The scale also acts as a regulatory factor on a larger, formal scale: it determines the order of word patterns in that the accent notes of words of more than one syllable result in an ascending F-sharp minor scale ("a-u-xi-li-um," accented note A, "me-um," accented note B etc). Monosyllabic words repeat the last note of the preceding word. The melodic line formed in this way is doubled in a parallel movement, whereby the interval between the two voices changes according to the pattern: sixth ("a-u-xi-li-um")—tenth ("me-um")—sixth ("a")—third ("Do-mi-ne")—sixth ("qui")—tenth ("fe-cit"), etc. Thus the individual settings of a particular word become part of a larger, ascending scalic motion: the musical panorama of a hilly landscape that rises into a mountain, analogous to the first verse of the psalm—"Levabo oculos ad montes" (I raise my eyes to the mountains).

Ex. 20

Chord progressions

From *Which was the Son of . . .* from the year 2000 onwards, alongside varied methods of melodic construction, we also find passages of polyphony which clearly are not based on the proliferation of an M-voice, but that are determined by chord progressions. Progressions formed by the transposition of a chord according to simple principles are to be found in earlier works, in *Hymn to a great city* (1984/2000) and in *Sieben Magnificat-Antiphinen* (1988/1991). In the first part of the seventh of the *Magnificat Antiphonen*—*O Immanuel*—the fifth-leap sequence leads a major triad through the entire circle of fifths and one step beyond (A–D–G–C–F–B-flat–E-flat–A-flat–D-flat–G-flat–B–E–A–D). The presence of all twelve notes of the chromatic scale offers a musical analogy to the omnipotence of Immanuel.

In *Hymn to a Great City* the fifth leap sequence is extended additively and moves only five steps through the circle of fifths, away from the G-sharp major triad to which it repeatedly returns (major triad on C-sharp–G-sharp/F-sharp–C-sharp–G-sharp/B–F-sharp–C-sharp–G-sharp/A–E–B–F-sharp–C-sharp–G-sharp). Counterbalancing the tonal uncertainty of such progressions that transcend the borders of keys, every two chords[80] a cadential formula D[7]-T in C-sharp major is added to the pedal point on G-sharp. In *O Immanuel* a T-voice is added to the upper notes of the chords which move through the entire cycle of fifths.

Such chord progressions move beyond the area of a particular key by strictly adhering to the sequence of major triads. However, in earlier works, chord progressions remain strictly within the borders set by the key. Characteristic of such progressions is the manner in which both basic elements of the tintinnabuli style—triad and scalic motion—are set in a different structural relationship to each other. The tintinnabuli triad does not unfold in a horizontal succession of notes, as in the T-voice, but, as with the traditional triad, is presented as a verticality, from which individual notes or pairs of notes are developed in stepwise motion.

Salve Regina is characterised by long stretches of three-note chord progressions. Apart from a few important exceptions, only two notes of each change successively at each chord change. First the lower two notes descend in stepwise motion then ascend to the original chord, then, symmetrically, the upper two notes ascend and descend. This results in an E-minor cadence with minor subdominant (s) and dominant (d) appearing in reversed order: (d) (t–d–t–s–t–s–T–s). It does not end however with the brighter major tonic (T instead of t), but with the minor subdominant (s), so that the preceding E-major Triad (T) acts as a major dominant to A-minor. The second phrase begins with a retrograde statement of the first, though from the third chord only the middle voice moves to the fourth. The C-major chord thus reached (in E-minor tG[81] to the tonic t) we reach a cadence in G-major, relative major to E-minor. At the end of the phrase the same pair of thirds moves in the upper voices back and forth as in the first phrase. However, in the lower voice is now the note D, leading these notes into the key of G-major. Through a chord change which involves stepwise move-

---

80 When the model is repeated, the cadential formula occurs every four bars.
81 German "Gegenklang," lit. "contrast chord." tG corresponds to chord VI in a minor key.

ment of all three notes of the chord, the repetition of both phrases returns to the opening two chords and thus back to E-minor (Ex. 21). In its implied and contradicting symmetries, its alternation between G and G-sharp, this seemingly simple chord progression differs from linear, stepwise thinking and, in its omission of a bass voice supporting the harmonic progression, subtly distances itself from the traditional cadential models from whose elements it is constructed.

Ex. 21

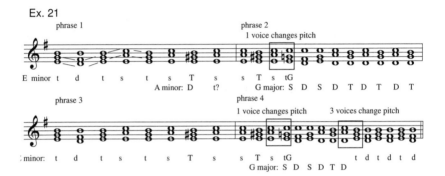

Decidedly simpler and entirely determined by symmetries is the chord progression in the three string passages of the section *Solitudine—stato d'animo*, from *Lamentate* (Ex. 22) for piano and orchestra. The three main degrees of A-flat minor (i–iv–V) are arranged symmetrically in a variety of ways. In retrograde symmetry A-flat minor s-t complements A-flat minor t-s. An inversion of the fourth leap follows with the closing tonic acting as static axis of symmetry (A-flat minor D-t t-D). Finally, in a retrograde statement of the progression, the second half leads back to the D-flat minor chord of the opening. The simplest tonal progressions are thus viewed from constantly shifting angles as if in a hall of mirrors and join to form an eight-bar group which is subdivided into four-bar units. A second bar supplements the first to form a two-bar phrase (a), a second phrase (b) supplements the first to form a four-bar period (A) followed by a balancing four bars.

Ex. 22

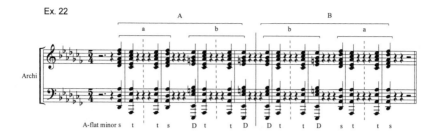

Chromatic Alteration

Chord progressions such as those quoted above represent a further facet of the interplay between triad and scale in the tintinnabuli style, enriching the relationship between M-voice and T-voice. The increasing importance of chromaticism results in a broadening of quite a different kind within the compositional techniques at Pärt's disposal—both through the integration of diminished seventh chords, and chromatic alteration of the historically familiar modal scales on which the M-voice was originally based.

Both weaken the pull of a tonal centre, which is at its strongest in the case of an unaltered diatonic scale with its tonic triad as tintinnabuli chord. Within the field of tension created by the tonally destabilising forces of diminished seventh chord and chromatically altered M-voice and the stabilising forces of tintinnabuli triad and pedal points, it falls more than ever to the strict structural relationships to connect and give various emphasis to these opposing tendencies. Within the overall formal process the influence of a single tonal centre is limited, in that various sections are not only structured differently but are in fact related to a variety of tonal centres.

Chromatic Alteration of the Melody

Already in *Fratres* (1977) we find the harmonic texture characterised by additional semitone steps in the M-voice resulting from chromatic alteration of a single note of the diatonic scale. In this piece the A-minor tintinnabuli triad and a drone in fifths are combined with the scale D–E–F–G–A–B-flat–C-sharp–D,[82] upon which the M-voice is based. In itself this would be a simple D-harmonic minor scale with two semitone steps and an augmented second. However, the tintinnabuli triad and the drone confirm the note A as tonic. Either the whole work is to be heard as a dominant preparation for a D-minor tonic that never actually sounds, or the scale is to be interpreted as A-phrygian, with an altered third note C-sharp (also known as phrygian major, Spanish, or Jewish scale) that alternates with the diatonic note C in the tintinnabuli triad: a state of harmonic hovering, emanating from the shimmering juxtaposition of C and C-sharp.[83]

As early as 1984, in the *Wallfahrtslied*, the chromatic scale makes a unique appearance, where it is bound to a tonal centre through the E-minor tintinnabuli triad. In the *Passacaglia* for violin and piano (2003), composed some 20 years later, chromatically ascending thirds in the upper voices combine with ascending major seconds in the bass. These outer voices—in themselves not bound to a tonic—are centred on A by the simultaneously sounding fifth A–E and the interpolated A-major/minor broken chords (Ex. 23). In this passacaglia no theme is repeated, instead the same chord progression, in the form of this funnel-shaped scalic contrary motion, repeats itself, extended across several octaves. It finally appears in retrograde, rounding off the formal process. Both the traditional passacaglia form and the opposition of tonality and atonality are thus preserved within the strictly structured framework of the piece.

Ex. 23

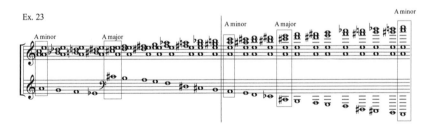

---

82 Versions of the piece with alternate instrumentation are transposed differently.

83 *Psalom* is based on the same scale transposed down a fourth. Due to the absence of a pedal-point the ambivalence between E-major (with phrygian second, F) and A-minor is more pronounced.

Most recently the descending chromatic scale has lent itself to the title of a short piece for piano trio from the year 2007: *Scala cromatica*.

The Diminished Seventh Chord

Very early on—in the closing section of *Tabula rasa* of 1977 discussed above— the diminished seventh chord appears as the opposing player to the tintinnabuli triad. It surfaces again in the outer instrumental sections of the *Wallfahrt-slied* in connection with chromatically diverging outer parts, and it appears in a variety of guises in the works from *Como cierva sedienta* (1998/2002) onwards. Both triad and diminished seventh chord alternate in *Von Angesicht zu Ange-sicht*. As a distortion of the triad with its stable perfect fifths, this juxtaposition offers a musical analogy of the text which contrasts our imperfect, shadowy understanding with an imagined perfect oneness, with a truth seen "face to face." On relatively rare occasions the diminished seventh chord replaces the triad as tintinnabuli chord altogether. In the fourth section of *Como cierva sedienta* (Figure H) two T-voices made up of the notes of the diminished seventh chord B–D–F–A-flat (8va -1/+1 and 8vab +1/-1) flank an M-voice centred on G' (Ex. 24): tonal disorientation as an expression of the desperate question to God, "¿Por qué me has olvidado?" ("Wherefore hast thou forsaken me?")

More frequently M-voices are led in parallel diminished seventh chords or, alternately, notes of the diminished seventh chord may be mixed with notes of the tintinnabuli triad. The *Spietato* section of the *Lamentate* (C) unites both of these devices and—for the first time in the tintinnabuli style— bases the M-voice on a quote: the Gregorian melody *Dies Irae*.

However, compared with the earlier *collage* works, the role of the musical quote has changed completely. In the earlier works quotes are intended as a contrast to the atonal sound world, taken out of context and as such identifiable and recognisable. In the latter work the quoted sequence is used as a pre-existant M-voice. No longer determined by the text, the M-voice becomes a sort of *cantus firmus*, similar to that in polyphonic music up to the 16th century, and the quote is thus absorbed into the tintinnabuli texture (Ex. 25). The notes of the chorale melody (C-sharp dorian) sound in the viola; the brass and solo piano add parallel tritoni below the chorale in regularly alternating octave positions, extending it to form notes of the G-sharp minor tintinnabuli triad (+1 and -1 to the notes of the tritonus interval). The eighth-note movement in upper strings completes the diminished seventh chord with a second tritonus and adds intervals of the tintinnabuli triad G-minor between both tritoni (bar 3 and 4). The superimposition and melodic interlocking of seventh chords and tintinnabuli triad create great harmonic tension, characterised by the omnipresence of the tritonus that relates the harmonic texture both to the melodic progression and to the textual content of the sequence (*Dies Irae = day of wrath*) in its description of the terrors of Judgement Day.

Ex. 25

La Sindone also begins with a tonal landscape that is rich in tensions characterised by parallel tritoni. They combine only in part to form a diminished seventh chord. Two voices at the interval of a 13th descend an E-minor scale with raised 4th and 7th degrees. Both voices are joined by a lower voice in parallel tritoni. The harmonies are further sharpened by the suspension of the upper voice into each subsequent chord, with the exception of the first and then every fifth, later every third note (Ex. 26). Sustained notes of the tintinnabuli triad E-minor in trombone, timpani, and double bass strengthen the reference to a tonic E. This tonic is thus present from the start, albeit in a weak form. Its confirmation at the end of the piece discussed above is tantamount to a musical revelation. The music outgrows its limits, breaking through its own barriers in a resurgent movement that brings it back to its starting point.

Ex. 26

In *Cantique des degrés* the diminished seventh chord fulfils yet another function. In the form of an ambiguous link belonging to eight different keys, it connects the tonal layers that change with each verse. The eight keys in which the diminished seventh chord D–F/E-sharp–A-flat/G-sharp–C-flat/B can resolve (E-flat major/minor, F-sharp major/minor, A-major/minor, C-major/minor) are allocated to the eight verses of the psalm so that the tonic of the keys, shifting constantly between major and minor, rises then falls in thirds. The circle of keys closes with the instrumental postlude in the opening key of E flat major.

Verse 1	Verse 2	Verse 3	Verse 4	Verse 5
E-flat major	F-sharp minor	A-major	C-minor	C-major

Verse 6	Verse 7	Verse 8	Postlude
A-minor	F-sharp major	E-flat minor	E-flat major

In *In principio*, a setting of the first 14 verses of St. John's Gospel for choir and orchestra, the diminished seventh chord is at first active only as a background structural device. In the first section it regulates the sequence of twelve major triads with added minor seventh in the bass that appear on all twelve degrees of the chromatic scale, relentlessly counteracting the unchanging A-minor triad in the choir in the form of instrumental interpolations. The descending bass/root notes of these chords result in three chromatically adjacent diminished seventh chords which make up the dodecaphonic total (Ex. 27). The uppermost voice ascends in contrary motion to the bass so that the chord opens out from close position in both directions.

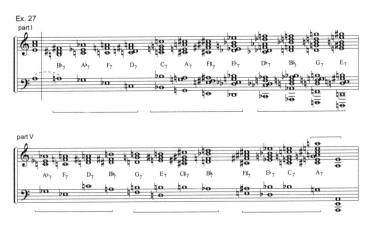

The text tells of a state of original being ("In principio erat verbum") from which a state of becoming emerges. In the music this all-embracing "becoming" corresponds to the continually expanding note sequence that encompasses all twelve notes. The unchanging A-minor triad represents the state of "being." Although the changing sequence of notes—an instrumental "becoming"—is opposed to the original "being" of the A-minor chord, it is related to it in two ways. The bass note of the first diminished seventh chord takes the root note of the chord, while the last diminished seventh chord acts as dominant (E) to the key of A-minor. However, it is not followed by an A-minor chord, but a rest, that may be seen as a refusal to follow the usual cadential progression at the end of the movement (E-major/A-minor = D-t). Once set in motion, the dynamic process that moves us away from this original state does and cannot lead back to the original A-minor—an embodiment of being, in which becoming is contained.

The final section (V) takes up the harmonic constellation of the first, the twelve seventh chords are given to the choir as it sings of "becoming" ("Et verbum caro factum est") and are grouped in such a way that the chords, transposed through adjacent semitones close with the A-major seventh chord. In the instrumental repetitions of the A-minor chord the third (C) is finally omitted and the final chord and its simultaneously sounding opposite—the pure fifth A–E—now merge. To continue the analogy: Being and Becoming, whose musical symbols are the fifth A–E and the diminished seventh chord on A, become one once more. The process of time, articulated in the dynamic, irreversible sequence of sounds, merges with the "Being" of the A-minor triad: we reach the end of musical time.

Coda

During the more than 30 years of tintinnabuli composition, the technical means of the style have been extended by new approaches, such as chord progression and additional material, such as chromaticism and diminished seventh chords. In addition, established rules regarding the setting of a text have undergone further differentiation. It is important to emphasise however that the fundamental aesthetic position of the style has not changed in any way. As these compositional means have grown more varied over the course of time, the challenge of unifying them has become greater. One might say that the radius of the musical means at the composer's disposal and of the technical methods of dealing with them has grown, while at the same time the challenge of grasping all these aspects from a central point, thus uniting even the points at opposite sides of the periphery has grown proportionally.

The circle seems to me to be a fitting image for the tintinnabuli style for another reason: its fascinating perfection is due to the simplicity of its appearance. Its simplicity and unity, directly perceptible through the senses, may be easily constructed geometrically. However, in calculating its dimensions one stumbles into the endless, a-periodic, irrational transcendent number π. So the circle may ultimately stand as a symbol for the way in which the clearly definable structural mechanisms of the tintinnabuli style, the rational process of planning, may be transformed into experiences beyond that which we can grasp rationally. In the simple mathematics of the tintinnabuli style, areas within and beyond the boundaries of rationality become interconnected.

Back to the Source

Saale Kareda

Saale Kareda, born in Tallinn in 1968, is a musicologist, freelance journalist, and translator. Since 2005 she has worked as cultural attachée to the Estonian Embassy in Vienna. From 1993–1999 she served as the music editor of the magazine *Teater.Muusika.Kino*. In 1998 she graduated with honours from the Estonian Music Academy in Tallinn. From 1999 she received a DAAD research grant in Berlin, and in 2000 a Herder-Preis-Stipendium in Vienna. From 2001–2007 she was employed by Universal Edition.

Kareda is currently studying for a doctorate at the University of Vienna with Prof. Gernot Gruber (*Algorhythmic and linguistically determined structures in the tintinnabuli style of Arvo Pärt*).

She is a member of the Estonian Musicology Society and the Estonian Composers' Guild.

One must look at the impossible until it becomes a simple matter.
Miracles are a question of practise.

Albert Einstein

"Every profound explanation of an empirical fact is nothing other than the confirmation of a miracle. The philologist occupies himself with the miracle of speech, the botanist with the miracle of plant life, the historian with the miracle of the course of the world: nothing but mysteries that no human has yet managed to decode. Even the physicist, if he is a genius, that is, constantly stumbles upon miracles."[84]

After a lot of hard "practise," a miracle—the tintinnabuli style—was indeed brought into the world in 1976 by the Estonian composer Arvo Pärt (born 1935). Since then, many tintinnabuli compositions have appeared. It is only with great difficulty that the existing tools of musicology try to analyse and classify the phenomenon of tintinnabuli (Pärt derived the name from the Latin word *tintinnabulum*, small bell). Attempts to pigeonhole the style with labels such as minimal music, new simplicity, or sacred minimalism are no longer *en vogue,* but we still find it hard to allocate an appropriate place for this style within our picture of the contemporary musical landscape.

Since the time of the enlightenment, modern man has increasingly lost the aspect of a vertical dimension in his thinking and feeling. At the time the tintinnabuli style came into being, the yearning for a lost sense of spirituality was very great, particularly behind the Iron Curtain. Through the music of Arvo Pärt, many people came to re-discover this lost vertical dimension, both at the time in the Soviet Union, and later throughout the world. While Pärt was persecuted in Estonia for his Christian beliefs, after his emigration to the West other accusations were levelled against him, such as that of the deliberate cultivation of the image of a mystic, a saint, and so on. Typical of an era ruled by boulevard journalism, Pärt's profound religious purpose was not evident to the average reporter. Since much in his music sounds provocatively simple, the tintinnabuli style has often been considered in the same light as mainstream minimal music. The receptive listener, however, is

---

84   Egon Friedell, *Kulturgeschichte der Neuzeit. Die Krisis der europäischen Seele von der schwarzen Pest bis zum ersten Weltkrieg* (Munich: Beck, 1969): 238.

intuitively aware of the exceptional spiritual concentration that lies behind its radically reduced means: a concentration capable of restoring a lost sense of our own spiritual dimension.

While Pärt is one of the most frequently performed contemporary composers, and his music is loved by a vast audience, many musicologists and critics find it difficult to accept his work. Boris Assafjew has pointed out the greater openness of the so-called ordinary listener: "The musician as specialist and the ordinary listener differ in one respect, namely that the first possesses a far greater store of ready-made, strictly systematic evaluations. The degree of prejudice in face of anything new does not necessarily decrease correspondingly with the specialist's greater knowledge. In fact exactly the opposite can happen: if he is unable to immerse himself in an unusual ways of thinking this prejudice can often grow. So strongly has he, in the practise of his musical profession, assimilated the accepted formulae and norms of music and its classifications, that they can make him lethargic."[85]

The mighty transformation of Pärt's work—the evolution from radical representative of the so-called Soviet avant-garde (he wrote the first dodecaphonic pieces in Estonia), through collage technique and an eight-year-long creative crisis, to the new tintinnabuli technique—this transformation is representative of the major shift in perspective that contemporary music in general has undergone, a metamorphosis that has proved Theodor Adorno's prognosis to be unjustified. Pärt's tintinnabuli compositions successfully demonstrate that a return to old, basic tonal cells is indeed legitimate, as long as the composer is able to re-structure these tonal atoms in a new way. Tintinnabuli music is a unique continuation of the technique of serial structuring, but the structural process is combined with a use of consonant tonal material. This is why it finds broad acceptance with its audience, "since the human ear may only perceive sound phenomena for which nature has constructed it."[86] According to harmonic Pythagoreanism, there exists an affinity among natural laws, the psycho-physical disposition of mankind, and music. In other words, a world-harmony with acoustic musical laws that can

---

85   Boris Assafjew, *Die musikalische Form als Prozeß*, ed. D. Lehmann and E. Lippold, (Berlin, Neue Musik 1976): 35.
86   Rudolf Haase, *Über das disponierte Gehör.* In *Fragmente als Beiträge zur Musiksoziologie*, Heft 4 (Vienna: Doblinger, 1977): 49ff.

be perceived by the human ear.[87] With the tintinnabuli style, Arvo Pärt has returned to this source.

Pärt tries to avoid mystic commentary about his compositional process, and in the rare cases when he does talk about his music, he concentrates on rational facts. He is here operating from a holistic view of the world that brings him much criticism, since scientists, philosophers, and artists with this holistic approach are a disregarded minority. Bertrand Russell once jokingly divided philosophers into those that believe the world to be a bowl of jelly, and those that believe it to be a bucket of shot. That is to say, those that believe that there is only one overall truth, and everything is part of this, and those that, like Wittgenstein, see the world as a complex of logically independent truths. Using concepts of William James, one may reduce this dichotomy to the simple contradiction between the "one" and the "many." Pärt belongs clearly to those who unrelentingly look for the "one," who share a vision of a unified truth on which the world is based. "The complex and many-faceted only confuses me, and I must search for unity," says Pärt, "But what is it, this one thing, and how do I find my way to it? Traces of this perfect thing appear in many guises and everything that is unimportant falls away. Tintinnabuli style is something like this."[88]

The search for sincerity, for the enduring, for the "one" that is the basis of all existence: this search has occupied Pärt since his early creative period. Already when he wrote *Credo* (1968), the work that led Pärt to the limits of his creative possibilities at that time, his basic artistic vision had already crystallised, as the following quote from an interview shows:

> It is said that many works of arts from earlier times appear to be more contemporary than works of today. This combination of "art" and "contemporary" is in itself absurd. However, what are we to make of this? Certainly not that a musical genius has a prophetic

---

87 The crisis of art music in the 20th century is thus seen as a result of a disregard of these harmonic principles: through numerous experimental approaches composers sought to discover how far music might be distanced from these original harmonic principles basic to all existence: a process very much in line with a modernistic view of humanity.

88 Wolfgang Sandner, booklet to CD *Tabula rasa*, ECM New series, ECM 1275 CD 817 764—2, Munich.

eye for future centuries. I think that the so-called contemporary nature of Bach's music will not disappear in the next 200 years, since, from an absolute point of view, it is simply of an integrally higher quality. The secret of this "contemporary" character lies not so much in how greatly the author embraces his time, but more in the way he perceives all of existence, with its joy, its suffering, and its experiences. It is more or less as if we tried to reduce a number (for example, one) in the form of an extremely complicated fraction with many intermediary calculations. The path to a solution is a tedious and strenuous process: however, the whole truth lies in reduction. If we assume that a similar solution (the number one) connects all the various fractions (epochs, human fates) then this one is more than the solution to a single fraction. It is the solution to all fractions (epochs, human fates), and it always has been. The limits of the single equation are too narrow, it moves through all of time. That means, the greater and clearer the recognition of this final solution (the number one), the more "contemporary" the work of art. Art should concern itself with the eternal, not the contemporary.[89]

As in the works of Anton Webern, in Pärt's tintinnabuli style reason and spirituality merge. Within this compositional style they are two sides of the same coin—although spirituality is treated with the greater regard by the composer. In this sense Webern and Pärt are similar in their creative processes: both approach the spiritual through mathematical formulae and convey irrational content through a rationalist compositional style. One might almost call them *rationalist mystics*, since both their lives' work consisted of penetrating deeply into the basic musical cell—the *Urzelle*—in an attempt to understand it and its relationship to the cells around it. A quote from a lecture that Webern gave in 1932 is of interest in connection with Pärt's music:

---

89   Arvo Pärt, quoted in Saale Kareda, "Dem Urknall entgegen: Einblick in den Tintinnabuli-Stil von Arvo Pärt", in: *Kirchenmusikalisches Jahrbuch* Jg. 84 (2000): 61. From the original Estonian in: "Merike Vaitmaa, Tintinnabuli—eluhoiak, stiil ja tehnika," *Teater. Muusika. Kina.* 7 (1988): 38.

It is for a later age to discover the minutiae of the laws that govern these works. If we arrive at a just view of art, then there can no longer be any difference between science and inspired creation. The further one looks, the more identical does everything become, and one finally has the impression that one is no longer looking at a human creation, but at nature.[90]

Tintinnabuli cells form a sort of web of sound from which, by means of invented or discovered mathematical algorithms, Pärt can create a variety of organisms. The compositional process of each work is largely limited to the invention of new algorithms. Though we may wonder, perhaps, whether the different formulae represent various facets of a primeval crystal, an *uralgorithm*, whether within the tintinnabuli style there are concealed structures that are fundamental to life itself—one cannot prove that any hidden structural world, more important than its apparent surface, exists behind the visible patternings of tintinnabuli music.

All seekers are looking to untangle the hidden codes behind the miracle of life. In the words of Nikolaus von Klues, "Though it can never be finally reached and understood, ultimate knowledge should not be regarded as unattainable, in the sense that all paths to it are blocked. Rather should we think of it as something we must continually approach, while in its absolute being it remains beyond our grasp."[91]

A faithful interpretation of tintinnabuli music creates intense fields of energy, or—if I may use a term of Andears Peer Kähler—"a radiating into silence," something that represents the most important quality of tintinnabuli music. Though some may try,[92] we cannot measure or analyse this dimension

---

90   Anton Webern, *Der Weg zur neuen Musik*, ed. W. Reich, (Vienna: Universal Edition, 1960): 60.
91   Nikolaus von Kues, "De visione Dei", 1453, in *Metzler Philosophen Lexikon. Von den Vorsokratikern bis zu den Neuen Philosophen*, ed. B. Lutz. (Stuttgart, J. B. Metzler, 1995): 633.
92   The works of Rupert Sheldrake offer an illuminating approach to the subject: his theory of morphogenetic fields is receiving increasing recognition in interdisciplinary debate. See Rupert Sheldrake's Theory of Morphogenetic Fields in Rupert Sheldrake, *Das schöpferische Universum. Die Theorie des morphogenetischen Feldes*, (Berlin, Ullstein Taschenbuch Verlag, 2008). Physicists speak of weak electronic fields (see also Giuliana Conforto, *Das Organische Universum*, [Potsdam, Mosquito Verlag 2006]).

of the music. Mainstream science lacks the surgical tools to dissect the intangible, the invisible, the limitless. It is much easier to repress this dimension, to deconstruct, to silence. However, this incomprehensible, hardly perceptible metaphysical aspect of our existence persists with an indestructible strength, and it speaks to those who are prepared to listen.

The works of Arvo Pärt represent a fearless and honest path on the search for a sense of spirit that has long since been banned from the modern world. In the deepest core of his being Arvo Pärt has discovered that place—a place in which he has found his way back to the source.

Two Acceptance Speeches

Arvo Pärt

Award Winners

Internationaler Brücke Prize Görlitz/Zgorzelec	Léonie-Sonning-Music Prize (Composers)
1993 Marion Gräfin Dönhoff	1959 Igor Stravinsky
1995 Adam Michnik	1965 Leonard Bernstein
1998 Jiri Grusa	1967 Witold Lutoslawski
1999 Freya von Moltke	1968 Benjamin Britten
2000 Arno Lustiger	1973 Dmitri Shostakovich
2001 Kardinal Miloslav Vlk	1977 Olivier Messiaen
2002 Wladyslaw Bartoszewski	1984 Miles Davis
2003 Kurt Biedenkopf	1985 Pierre Boulez
2004 Valdas Adamkus	1990 György Ligeti
2005 Giora Feidman	1996 Per Nørgård
2007 Arvo Pärt	1999 Sofia Gubaidulina
2008 Fritz Stern	2003 György Kurtág
2009 Norman Davies	2008 Arvo Pärt

Acceptance Speech Given on the Occasion of the International
Brücke Prize of the European City of Görlitz 2007,
November 9th, 2007

Dear Guests, Dear Friends,

It is an unusual business for a musician to be standing here, the centre of attention for politicians and scientists. I hear words about my music and my person that sound, to my ears, somewhat exaggerated, since I never set myself such grandiose goals as those you speak of here. My goals and standards are much more modest, and a lot simpler. At the time when my present music came into existence I had my hands full just trying to solve my own problems. I had to put myself into a state of mind which would allow me to discover a musical language that I could live with. I was in search of a little island of sound. In search of a place in my innermost being where—shall we say—a dialogue with God might take place. Finding this place became a task of vital importance for me.

I am sure that such a need is felt—consciously or unconsciously—by every one; and perhaps many of you know this, know what I am talking about, already.

To illustrate my thoughts I would like to offer you a picture: if we look at any substance through an electron microscope, a magnification of a thousand will obviously look very different from that of a million. But if we move slowly through all the possible gradients of magnification we may discover unimaginable, fairly chaotic landscapes. Yet, at some point there is a border—somewhere in the region of a magnification of thirty million. Here all the fantastic landscapes disappear and we see a strict geometry, a sort of network, very clear and very special. What is surprising is the fact that this geometry looks very similar, even in very different substances.

Is something like this true of human beings?

Let us fantasise. Let us attempt to examine a human soul as if it were under such a microscope, gradually increasing the degree of magnification. We will witness how all the superficial features of a human being—his particular characteristics, all his virtues and weaknesses—disappear more and more from the image as the magnification increases. It will be like an endless process of reduction, which leads us towards the bare essentials. On this "journey into the interior" we leave behind all social, cultural, political, and religious contexts. In the end we arrive at a net-like basic pattern. We might call it a *human geometry*, clearly organized, peacefully shaped—and above all: beautiful.

At this depth we are all so similar that we could recognize ourselves in each other. And this level may be the only place where a practicable bridge of peace is conceivable: where all our problems—if indeed they still exist here—might be solved.

For me it is a great temptation to see this well-ordered, fundamental substance, this precious island of the soul's seclusion, as the place of which it was said 2000 years ago, *here is the Kingdom of God*—namely within ourselves. Irrespective of whether we are old or young, rich or poor, woman or man, coloured or white, talented or less talented. And so, to this day, I try to stay on that path in search of this long-awaited magic island, where all people—for me, all sounds—can live in peace with one another. The doors to this place are open to all of us. But the path towards it is difficult—difficult to the point of despair.

Your Brücke Prize gives me new strength, and encourages me to carry on along this path.

Many thanks,
Arvo Pärt

Acceptance Speech on Occasion of the Presentation of the Léonie-Sonning-Music Prize 2008, on May 22nd, 2008, in Copenhagen

Dear Members of the Prize Committee, Dear Friends,

We have to admit: man is an imperfect being. There is no piece of knowledge about himself that man accepts with so much difficulty and reluctance. Perhaps some people believe that a composer is an exception. I have to say to you: no, he is not—unfortunately.

"But what is perfection?" we may ask—in reference to the famous question of Pilatus. And, if we really did have the answer to hand, would it help us? Because at first sight it seems as if the concept of perfection has little place in our everyday lives. Somehow it isn't up to date, no longer relevant today. However, in the creative process of the artist, this "eternal question" appears in all its weight and urgency. It give the creator no peace. It drives him on, because with body and soul he longs for this perfection. Almost to the point of desperation, he searches for that which he desires so intensely.

Too often the goals he sets for himself are beyond his own abilities. And this disparity makes him painfully aware of his limitations. But sometimes such extreme efforts can lead to results that exceed even the limits of the author himself, the limits of what he is capable of. Then something happens that does not obey the laws of logic. A work emancipates itself from the unpropitious conditions of its creation. One might say: in such a case a successful work can be much better than its creator. It swings itself up above him and his earthly imperfection. The new dimension of his work—even if it is still far from perfect—is in a position to overcome the human imperfection of its author.

We can sometimes see something comparable in the field of athletics. A record! Although this doesn't happen every day—and although perhaps one day it will be exceeded by someone else, or by the sportsman himself—a very special moment has occurred and something of lasting value has come into being. Isn't it the case that awards mark such special moments? Anyway, that is the way I see it in my case. The prize, this big prize, honours, in my eyes, a music that exceeds my capabilities as man and musician. And so allow me in the name of some of my works to thank the Léonie Sonning Music Prize committee with all my heart. Both of us, my music and I, are overjoyed to be able to carry the title of Léonie Sonning Award Winner.

Many thanks,
Arvo Pärt

Selected Discography

Tabula rasa, ECM New Series 1275
Fratres (violin and piano) • Cantus in Memory of Benjamin Britten • Fratres (celli) • Tabula rasa
Gidon Kremer, Keith Jarrett; Tatjana Grindenko, Alfred Schnittke, Staatsorchester Stuttgart, Dennis Russell Davies; Lithuanian Chamber Orchestra, Saulus Sondeckis

Arbos, ECM New Series 1325
Arbos • An den Wassern zu Babel • Pari intervallo • De profundis • Es sang vorlangen Jahren • Summa • Stabat Mater
Christopher Bowers-Broadbent, organ; Hilliard Ensemble; Brass Ensemble Staatsorchester Stuttgart, Dennis Russell Davies

Passio, ECM New Series 1370
Passio Domini nostri Jesu Christi secundum Joannem
Hilliard Ensemble, Paul Hillier

Miserere, ECM New Series 1430
Miserere • Festina lente • Sarah Was Ninety Years Old
Hilliard Ensemble, Paul Hillier; Orchester der Beethovenhalle Bonn, Dennis Russell Davies

Te Deum, ECM New Series 1505
Te Deum • Silouan's Song • Magnificat • Berliner Messe
Estonian Philharmonic Chamber Choir, Tallinn Chamber Orchestra, Tõnu Kaljuste

Litany, ECM New Series 1592
Litany • Psalom • Trisagion
Hilliard Ensemble; Tallinn Chamber Orchestra, Estonian Philharmonic Chamber Choir, Tõnu Kaljuste; Lithuanian Chamber Orchestra, Saulius Sondeckis
ECM New Series 1592

Collage, CHANDOS 9134
Collage sur B-A-C-H • Summa (string orchestra) • Wenn Bach Bienen gezüchtet hätte • Fratres (string orchestra) • Symphony N° 2 • Festina lente • Credo
Boris Berman, piano; Philharmonia Orch. & Chorus, Neeme Järvi

Arvo Pärt, BIS CD 434
Cello Concerto "Pro et contra" • Perpetuum mobile • Symphony N° 1 • Symphony N° 2 • Symphony N° 3
Bamberg Symphony Orchestra, Neeme Järvi

De Profundis, Harmonia Mundi HMU 907 182
De profundis • Missa syllabica • Solfeggio • And One of the Pharisees • Cantate Domino • Summa • 7 Magnificat Antiphonen • The Beatitudes • Magnificat
Theatre of Voices, Paul Hillier

Summa, BIS-CD 834
Cantus in Memory of Benjamin Britten • Collage über B-A-C-H • Festina lente • Fratres (string orchestra) • Summa (string orchestra) • Tabula rasa
Tapiola Sinfonietta, Jean-Jacques Kantorow

Beatus, ECM New Series 1654/55
Statuit ei Dominus • Missa syllabica • Beatus Petronius • 7 Magnificat-Antiphonen • De profundis • Ode VII (Memento) from Kanon Pokajanen • Cantate Domino • Solfeggio
Estonian Philharmonic Chamber Choir, Tõnu Kaljuste

Kanon Pokajanen, VIRGIN Classics 7243 5 45276
Estonian Philharmonic Chamber Choir, Tõnu Kaljuste

Alina, ECM New Series 1591
Für Alina • Spiegel im Spiegel
Vladimir Spivakov, Sergej Bezrodny, Dietmar Schwalke, Alexander Malter

I Am the True Vine, Harmonia Mundi HMU 907242
Bogoróditse dyévo • I Am the True Vine • Ode IX (Nïnye k vam) from Kanon Pokajanen • The Woman with the Alabaster Box • Tribute to Caesar • Berliner Messe (choir and organ)
Christopher Bowers-Broadbent, Theatre of Voices, The Pro Arte Singers, Paul Hillier

Orient Occident, ECM New Series 1795
Wallfahrtslied/Pilgrims' Song • Orient & Occident • Como cierva sedienta
Swedish Radio Symphony Orchestra, Swedish Radio choir, Tõnu Kaljuste

Triodion, Hyperion CDA67375
Dopo la vittoria • My Heart's in the Highlands • Triodion • I am the true vine • Littlemore Tractus • Which was the son of . . . • Nunc dimittis • Salve Regina
Polyphony, David James, Christopher Bowers-Broadbent, Stephen Layton

Stabat Mater, ATMA Classique ACD2 2310
Psalom (string quartet) • Summa • Fratres (string quartet) • Es sang vor langen Jahren • Summa (violin, 2 viola, cello) • Stabat mater
Daniel Taylor, Quatour Franz Joseph, Studio de musique ancienne de Montréal,
Christopher Jackson

Spiegel im Spiegel, BIS CD 1434
Cantus in Memory of Benjamin Britten • Fratres (violin and piano) • Dopo la vittoria • Bogoróditse Djévo • I am the True Vine • Annum per Annum • Spiegel im Spiegel (violin and piano) • Variationen zur Gesundung von Arinuschka • Quintettino • Concerto Piccolo über B-A-C-H • Fratres (string quartet)

Arvo Pärt—A Tribute, Harmonia Mundi HMU 907407
Dopo la vittoria • Bogoróditse dyévo • I Am the True Vine • The Woman with the Alabaster Box • Which was the son of • Berliner Messe (choir and organ) • Solfeggio • Magnificat
Estonian Philharmonic Chamber Choir, Christopher Bowers-Broadbent, Theatre of Voices, The Pro Arte Singers, Paul Hillier

Lamentate, ECM New Series 1930
Lamentate • Da Pacem Domine
SWR RSO Stuttgart, Alexei Lubimov, Andrey Boreyko, Hilliard Ensemble

Da Pacem, Harmonia Mundi HMU 807401
Da pacem Domine • Salve Regina • 2 Slawische Psalmen • Magnificat • An
den Wassern zu Babel • Dopo la vittoria • Nunc dimittis
Estonian Philharmonic Chamber Choir, Christopher Bowers-Broadbent,
Paul Hillier

In Principio, ECM New Series 2050
In Principio • La Sindone • Cecilia vergine romana • Da Pacem Domine •
Mein Weg • Für Lennart in Memoriam
Estonian National Symphony Orchestra, Estonian Philharmonic Chamber
Choir, Tallinn Chamber Orchestra, Tõnu Kaljuste

Symphony No. 4, ECM New Series 2160
Symphony No. 4 "Los Angeles" • Kanon Pokajanen (Fragments)
Los Angeles Philharmonic, Esa-Pekka Salonen
Estonian Philharmonic Chamber Choir , Tõnu Kaljuste

Cantique, Sony Classical 88697723342
Stabat Mater • Symphony No. 3 • Cantique des degrés
Rundfunksinfonieorchester Berlin, RIAS Kammerchor, Kristja Järvi

Pilgrim's Song, ERP 2309
Ein Wallfahrtslied • Magnificat • Summa • Nunc Dimittis • Te Deum
Chamber Choir Voces Musicales, Tallinn Sinfonietta, Risto Joost

Creator Spiritus, Harmonia Mundi HMU 807553
Veni creator • The Deer's Cry • Psalom • Most Holy Mother of God • Solfeggio • My Heart's in the Highlands • Peace upon you, Jerusalem • Ein Wallfahrtslied • Morning Star • Stabat Mater

Theatre of Voices, Ars Nova Copenhagen, Paul Hillier
Adam's Lament, ECM New Series 2225 (to be released in November 2012)
Adam's Lament • Beatus Petronius • Salve Regina • Statuit ei Dominus • Alleluia-Tropus • L'Abbé Agathon • Estnisches Wiegenlied • Weihnachtliches Wiegenlied
Tallinn Chamber Orchestra, Riga Sinfonietta, Latvian Radio Choir, Vox Clamantis, Estonian Philharmonic Chamber Choir, Tõnu Kaljuste

ARVO PÄRT was born in 1935 in Paide, Estonia. Working first through the major compositional techniques of the twentieth-century avant-garde, Pärt found his own unique voice in the mid-seventies—striving not for complexity, but a limitation to the essential. Pärt is one of the most profound and acclaimed composers living today.

DR. ROBERT JAMIESON CROW teaches musicology at the Universities of Salzburg and Innsbruck, and his compositions have been performed throughout Europe and in the US.